▼ FOCUS ON IELTS

IELTS

Teacher's Book

W9-CFG-492

SUE O'CONNELL

Pearson Education Limited
Edinburgh Gate, Harlow
Essex CM20 2JE, England
and Associated Companies throughout the world

www.pearsonelt.com

First published 2010

Third impression 2012

Set in 10/12pt Times New Roman

Printed in Malaysia, KHL-CTP

978-1-4082-3917-9

Designed by Jennifer Coles

New edition by Ken Vail Graphic Design

Cover images: *Front:* **Photolibrary.com:** fstop/Holger Hill

▶ Contents

▶ Introduction

Welcome to *Focus on IELTS* new edition! Whether you are a first time user or an old *Focus* hand, we hope you find everything you and your students need in the course, and that you enjoy working on it together.

Focus on IELTS new edition provides comprehensive preparation for the Listening and Speaking modules and the Academic Reading and Writing modules of the IELTS Test. It is designed to build students' confidence and proficiency through systematic skills development and graded exam practice.

While retaining all the key features from the original course, this updated version has an increased focus on academic skills, which will equip your students with the tools they need for success not only in the IELTS test but also in their future studies.

These notes will guide you through the various components, including the important new academic strand. You will find detailed teaching notes, keys to exercises in the units and recording scripts for the recordings.

Key features of *Focus on IELTS* new edition

*   New **Reflective Learning** and **Critical Thinking** training develops students' analytical skills and enables them to become more independent learners.

*   New **Academic Style** sections focus on key aspects of academic English and help students to write in an appropriate style.

*   New **Academic Vocabulary** sections systematically build up students' knowledge of the all-important *Academic Word List*.

*   **Exam Briefing** boxes and **Task Approach** contain essential information and advice about IELTS modules and tasks.

*   Regular **Error Hit Lists** help students eliminate common errors from their work.

*   The **Key Language Bank** provides reference material and extra practice to help students increase their vocabulary and consolidate key grammar.

*   An expanded **Writing Practice Bank** provides example answers for selected questions and additional writing practice.

*   An interactive **iTest** on the CD-ROM provides additional exam practice.

Structure

The book begins with an *Overview* of the IELTS Test. This provides at-a-glance information about the overall organisation of the exam as well as details of the four modules, including the assessment criteria used in marking.

There are twenty units, divided into pairs under ten general topic headings. Each unit begins with an outline of the main practice activities and the relevant exam focus. Odd-numbered units (1, 3, etc.) focus mainly on reading, while even numbered units (2, 4, etc.) focus mainly on listening and writing. Each pair of units also includes speaking practice.

Between units there are additional practice sections suitable for class or self-study. These include *Error Hit Lists,* and the **academic skills strand**: *Academic Style, Academic Vocabulary, Critical Thinking* and *Reflective Learning*. There is more information about these sections under **Unit Contents**.

The end section of the book contains a range of supplementary practice material in the *Key Language Bank* and the *Writing Practice Bank*. There are also *Answer keys* to selected exercises in the units and to the *Reflective Learning, Critical Thinking, Key Language* and *Writing Practice Bank* exercises.

For full details of the contents, see the *Map of the book* on pages 2–4 of the Student's Book.

How to use the course

The material has been designed to be as flexible as possible so that the time needed to work through the course can be expanded or contracted, depending on the level of the students and the contact hours available. Similarly, students can do more or less work outside class depending on their circumstances and individual needs.

Fast-track route

The minimum time needed to complete the course is about 60 hours. In this case, students will need to work through most of the exercises in the **academic skills strand** in their own time and also use the *Key Language Bank* and the *Writing Practice Bank* as self-access resources. Some of the written work from the units will need to be set for homework and it may also be helpful if students tackle some of the longer reading tasks before the lesson so that class time can be most productively spent in task analysis.

More extended courses

If time is not at a premium and most of the work (including relevant supplementary practice exercises) is done in class time, the material could easily occupy 100+ hours.

Structure

The exam *Overview* on page 5 is a good starting point for the course because it gives students a clear indication of the goal they are aiming at. It can then become a regular reference point as students become more concerned about the exact requirements of the IELTS test.

With an exam as challenging as IELTS, it's particularly important to capitalise on what students can do for themselves. The *Reflective Learning* sections are designed to play an important role in this by helping students to become more independent learners. It's important to reinforce this message by encouraging them to make use of good dictionaries and grammar books, as well as the many resources within this book, including the *Error Hit Lists*, and the exercises in the **academic skills strand**. In addition, they should become familiar with the *Key Language Bank* and *Writing Practice Bank* at an early stage so they can use them for individualised practice.

Unit contents

Lead-in

The *Lead-in* sections serve as an introduction to the topic and a foundation for the activities in the unit. They allow students to share any experience or knowledge they may have, to practise a variety of communicative skills, and to extend their range of topic vocabulary. Activities include a wide range of discussion topics, quizzes, and problem-solving tasks.

Focus on reading

One of the main challenges of the Academic Reading module of the IELTS test is the length of the passages, and it's important that students have plenty of exposure to extended texts in order to develop the skills and confidence needed to deal with them. For this reason, the ten main texts reflect IELTS requirements in terms of content and length. On very intensive courses, this may mean that some reading tasks have to be set for homework. However, there are also a number of shorter texts with tasks designed to practise specific reading skills, which can easily be completed in class time.

The reading texts come from a variety of sources including books, journals and newspapers, and represent different styles and approaches. A full range of reading skills is practised, and each of the main exam task types, is introduced in *Exam Briefing* boxes, while clear strategies for dealing with individual questions are set out in *Task Approach* sections.

Focus on writing

There is thorough preparation for both tasks in the Academic Writing module, and the skills required are built up from sentence level, with an emphasis on appropriate linking and clear paragraphing. Each task is introduced in an *Exam Briefing* box, and there is advice on approaching specific topics in the *Task Approach* sections.

For Task 1, students are trained in interpreting information from graphs, charts and tables, and in describing objects and explaining processes. There is also step-by-step practice in producing an effective answer for Task 2, including analysing the question, structuring an argument, presenting supporting points and writing summarising sentences.

The *Writing Practice Bank* at the end of the book contains model answers for selected tasks, guided practice tasks and additional exam topics.

Focus on listening

The twenty listening texts provide balanced coverage of the four sections of the Listening module and represent a wide variety of speech situations, both formal and informal. The recordings follow the IELTS practice of featuring different varieties of English, including Irish and American, as well as Australian and British. The recording scripts are reproduced at the end of this book.

There are introductions to the four sections of the test and to general task-types such as completion and labelling a diagram/plan/map in *Exam Briefing* boxes, while clear strategies for dealing with individual questions are set out in the *Task Approach* sections.

Focus on speaking

Students need a wide range of speaking skills in order to do well in the Speaking module. They have to be able to talk about familiar personal matters and general topics in Parts 1 and 2, as well as discussing more abstract issues in Part 3. Among other things, they may need to provide information, express and justify opinions, compare and contrast, and speculate. In doing so, they must demonstrate fluency and coherence, an adequate range of vocabulary and grammar, and acceptable pronunciation.

This is a tall order, requiring thorough preparation in terms of both language and confidence. For this reason, the book provides ample opportunity for motivating oral practice, not only in the *Focus on speaking* sections, but also in *Lead-ins* and elsewhere. Early units feature a wide variety of speaking activities involving pair or group discussion. Later units move to more exam focused practice leading to a complete practice interview in Unit 20.

Each of the three parts of the Speaking module is introduced in an *Exam Briefing* box, and the *Useful language* boxes provide support for individual activities as well as building a reliable repertoire of essential basic structures.

Focus on vocabulary

For success in IELTS, students need to acquire an adequate working vocabulary in order to express themselves, on a range of topics and issues, from the personal to the more general and abstract. They also need to be able to cope with the wide and unpredictable range of unknown words that they will meet in academic reading texts.

Both these areas are addressed in the *Focus on vocabulary* sections and there is an emphasis throughout on systematic vocabulary-building through the use of word families and other techniques. There is also specific training in working out the meaning of unknown words, using clues from the context, and/or from elements of a word such as prefixes and suffixes.

Some vocabulary sections include pronunciation practice focusing on aspects of word stress and sounds. Make a point of explaining how the value of this, not only for its relevance to speaking skills, but also because of the important role it plays in improving listening skills.

NB There is additional vocabulary practice in the ten *Academic Vocabulary* sections, and in the *Key Language Bank,* which contains sixteen vocabulary exercises including word building, collocations and topic vocabulary.

Error Hit Lists

There are ten *Error Hit Lists*, one after each pair of units. These draw on the *Longman Learner's Corpus* and target the most common errors of grammar or vocabulary relevant to the topic or tasks in the units. Examples include the difference in meaning and use between *possibility* and *opportunity* or between *economic* and *economical*.

Error Hit Lists are intended as an active learning resource for students, and it's worth taking time at the beginning of the course to explain exactly what they are and how to make best use of them. In all, there are thirty-eight language points covering around ninety separate expressions. If students make a point of studying and revising each *Error Hit List* systematically as the course progresses, they should be able to eliminate a significant number of the most common and predictable errors from their written and spoken English.

It would be helpful to have regular spot checks and to include other revision work based on the *Error Hit Lists*. Language points from the *Error Hit Lists* are also revised through occasional *Spot the Error* exercises.

The academic skills strand

This consists of four components: *Academic Style, Academic Vocabulary, Reflective Learning,* and *Critical Thinking.* There are thirty sections in all, located between units. These are colour-coded in the Map of the Book on pages 2–4 and the study pages have matching coloured bands for easy identification. There are keys to the exercises on pages 256–259 of the Student's Book,

enabling students to use these sections for self-study if appropriate.

Academic Style and Academic Vocabulary

These sections are designed to raise students' awareness of important aspects of academic language. They occur as a pair every two units, and the pages have purple coloured bands.

Academic Style: ten sections focusing on key features of academic writing including functions, formality and hedging, as well as the use of grammatical structures which play an important role in academic texts such as the passive and noun phrases. An awareness of these features will not only enable students to read more efficiently by making the relation between ideas in a text clearer, but will also help them write in an appropriate style.

Academic Vocabulary: ten sections focusing on key vocabulary from the *Academic Word List* (AWL), a list of the most common words in academic texts. This is a very valuable resource which makes it possible to target the key vocabulary students need in order to improve their reading and writing in the IELTS test. There is more information about the AWL on page 208 and it would be helpful for students to study this before they tackle to the first *Academic Vocabulary* section. There is a reference list of all the words included in the *Academic Vocabulary* sections on pages 208–209.

Reflective Learning and Critical Thinking

These sections occur every four units. They introduce students to study strategies and ways of approaching academic tasks which will help them learn as effectively as possible. The activities work best as pair or group discussion with teacher support but the key in the Student's book means they can also be used for self-study if necessary on more intensive courses.

Reflective Learning: five sections, identifiable by green coloured bands. This academic strand will help students develop the skills needed for learner autonomy, one of the key requirements for successful learning. Once students develop the ability to function independently as learners they will learn more effectively, make faster progress and, crucially, go on learning outside the classroom and after the course has finished. This is particularly important for international students, who may receive limited (or no) language support during their academic studies.

The *Reflective Learning* activities are designed to make students more aware of factors that help or hinder successful learning, and to help them choose appropriate learning strategies, set personal learning goals and monitor their own progress. For each topic, students assess their current performance, set a realistic learning goal. In the next section, they review progress towards this goal in a **Plan/Do/Review** cycle.

Critical Thinking: five sections, identifiable by orange coloured bands. Critical thinking is a way of careful analytical thinking that is needed in all parts of the IELTS test, for example to evaluate an argument in a reading text or to analyse a writing topic and plan an appropriate answer. This academic strand is designed to help students engage actively and constructively in tasks and to form independent opinions based on relevant evidence. These skills will not only improve students' performance in IELTS tasks but also stand them in good stead for their future academic studies.

Practice banks

The two practice banks contain supplementary language and writing exercises which can be used in a number of ways, depending on the time available and students' needs. With lower-level students on more extended courses, you may choose to include most of these exercises in class time. With higher-level students on intensive courses, the exercises can be treated purely as self-access resources. In all other cases, they can be used as and when the need arises, for example for homework, for revision/remedial teaching, to meet the needs of a specific student, or, in the case of vocabulary tasks, as convenient 'fillers' between other segments of a lesson.

All the *Key language* and *Writing practice* exercises are cross-referenced to the relevant unit.

- The *Key Language Bank* contains thirty-four supplementary exercises focusing on grammar and vocabulary. The keys to all the *Key language* exercises can be found on pages 260–262 of the Student's Book.

- The *Writing Practice Bank* contains twenty supplementary writing exercises, including example answers, guided practice exercises and additional exam topics. The keys to the guided-practice exercises of the *Writing Practice Bank* can be found on page 262–263 of the Student's Book.

1 ▶ Health's 'magic bullet'

To set the ball rolling ...

With books closed, write up the expression 'magic bullet', perhaps giving a couple of examples: *There is no magic bullet for weight loss. Currency devaluation is not a magic bullet to lift the country out of recession.* See if students know or can guess what it means. Explain that the term comes originally from medical research where it described a drug that killed only the particular organism that was targeted, e.g. cancer cells. It was invented by the German scientist Paul Ehrlich who won the Nobel prize for his work on chemotherapy. It's now used more generally to mean a 'quick fix' to a problem.

Ask what 'Health's magic bullet' might be and establish that it's simply exercise. NB This is mentioned in text C on page 10. Point out that physical activity is a common topic in the IELTS exam, both for speaking or writing. If you have time you could outline some typical aspects of the subject on the board – see example below. This is a good way of establishing a clear exam focus from the outset.

TOPIC: PHYSICAL ACTIVITY
PERSONAL EXPERIENCE

(Speaking parts 1 and 2)

- **What leisure activities ...**
- *– do you do regularly?*
- *– are popular in your country?*
- **What sport(s) ...**
- *– do you take part in?*
- *– do you enjoy watching*
- **How do you keep fit?**

GENERAL DISCUSSION POINTS

(Speaking part 3; Writing Task 2)

- *What are the health benefits of exercise?*
- *How can we encourage people to take more exercise?*
- *Should the government subsidise public sports facilities?*
- *What do children learn through playing team sports?*
- *What is the appeal of dangerous sports like free climbing?*

Lead-in *(p.8)*

1 Explain that statements 1–5 contain facts about the topic of physical activity and that there are two missing numbers in each one. The task is to select the correct pair of figures from the box to complete each statement. Arrange students in pairs to discuss and complete the task.

2 Once students have checked answers on page 253, have a class discussion based on questions 1–3. Draw their attention to the word *activity* and elicit the verb and adjective *activate*, *active* and opposites *inactive*, *inactivity*. Point out that learning the other members of a word family like this is a very effective way of building vocabulary. It's also worth focusing on the use of collocations with *do* and *play*, e.g. *do a sport/ do exercise*, *play tennis/football*. See notes in *Error Hit List*, page 26.

Focus on speaking 1 *Talking about personal interests (p.9)*

Read through the *Exam Briefing* as a class, and answer any general questions students have about this aspect of the exam.

Invite students to ask you one or two of the bullet point questions first, so you can demonstrate the use of some target language in a suitably full answer, e.g. *Well, the thing I really hate is going to the gym. I know it's good for me, but I just find it so boring!*

It's worth spending some time on the *Useful language* because this includes some very common and useful expressions. Focus on some key grammatical patterns and practise as necessary, e.g.

to go + -ing, e.g. *go running/jogging/swimming,* etc. (See notes in *Error Hit List*, page 26.)

verbs followed by noun/-ing, e.g. *love/enjoy/hate/can't stand* football/watching football, etc.

cleft sentences: The thing ... is ..., e.g. *The thing I want to know is ...*

to find (something) + adjective, e.g. *I find chess really fascinating.*

Draw students' attention to the way answers can be made fuller by including time expressions, and by giving reasons. Finally, focus on the use of fluency markers.

Let students work in pairs to interview each other. Monitor the conversations and round off by asking a few students to report back on what their partner said. Doing this on a regular basis tends to encourage better listening!

Focus on reading 1 *Text types (p.9)*

This is an important concept for students to understand and is the basis for the *Academic Style* sections in the book.

As a brief introduction, ask students to name some different kinds of writing, e.g. *a personal letter, a newspaper article, a text message, a novel,* etc., and pick two or three to compare. Ask what would be different about the style in each case, if necessary us prompts such as *Formal or informal language? Complete sentences or notes? Complete words or abbreviations?*, etc.

1 Let students work individually to read the extracts before comparing answers in pairs. When checking answers, ask them to say which features of style helped them identify the text types.

2 These questions are best discussed as a class. Explain that a language function is a writer's purpose in writing. NB Functions are examined in more detail in *Academic Style 1*, page 16. Ask students to identify language which expresses the functions of:
persuasion (D), e.g. the use of superlatives and other very positive expressions *most advanced, top quality, excellence*
evidence and conclusions (B), e.g. topic vocabulary *study ... conducted, results revealed ..., differences observed;* (C) *studying, researchers, a result*

3/4 Students could usefully work together on these tasks. Exercise 3 focuses on some basic aspects of style while exercise 4 summarises the key features of academic English. Make sure students have a correct version of exercise 4 for future reference. Point out that recognising functions and their associated features of style is an important reading skill, and will also help improve their academic writing.

Focus on speaking 2 *Comparing and contrasting (p.11)*

1 Read through the introduction as a class and tell students to study the *Useful language*. Then ask them to look at the two photographs and suggest a few differences between the two activities.

2 Let students complete the dialogue and compare answers. For further practice of the target language, ask them to compare the following pairs:

- swimming in a pool vs swimming in the sea
- tennis vs golf
- a novel vs a textbook
- TV vs cinema

They should make similar statements to the ones in the dialogue. Use the first pair as an example, supplying suitable prompt words, e.g. *Both ...?, But ...?, For example ...?* You could also ask students to write up one or more comparisons as a record and to underline relevant language.

3 Questions 1–3 are examples of exam discussion topics which call for comparisons. Point out that it's important to extend your answers if possible by giving reasons for opinions and by mentioning any personal experience you may have, e.g. *The last time I travelled by train, the heating broke down and we arrived twenty minutes late.* Monitor discussions and provide appropriate feedback afterwards.

Focus on reading 2 *The walking school bus (p.12)*

1 Read through the *Exam Briefing* as a class, and let students study the notes on the three reading skills. As reinforcement, you could ask them which skills they would use to:
a) read the information about a university course you are considering taking. (reading for detail)
b) find their exam results in a long list of candidates. (scanning)
c) look at an article on the internet and decide whether to print it off. (skimming)

Take a moment to consider general reading strategies, which students will no doubt know about, but which are worth reviewing. Say you are going to make a number of statements about reading in the IELTS exam, and that for each one they must say *Do*, if it is good advice, or *Don't* if it is not.

- Read the whole text in detail first. (Don't. This is unnecessary and wastes time.)
- Look at the heading, if there is one, and read through text. (Do. This will help you form a general picture of the content.)
- Study the questions carefully. (Do. This will enable you to identify sections of the text you need to read carefully, and tell you what information to look for.)
- Try to understand every word. (Don't. This is a waste of time if the word is not essential to understanding. If it is an important word, try to rough guess the meaning.)

2 Remind students about text types (see *Focus on reading 1*). Before they look through the text, ask them to study the four options carefully, and suggest a few features of style they might expect in each one. It may be helpful to set a time limit, say 3 minutes for reading, to underline the need to skim-read rather than read intensively.

Let them compare answers, and discuss the stylistic features which helped them choose the correct option such as fairly formal vocabulary, e.g. *significant decline, thus* (A)*, designated location* (B)*, furthermore* (F); use of passive constructions, e.g. *It has been suggested* (B)*, it was reported* (F); the inclusion of detailed statistics, e.g. (D); and references to research findings, e.g. *Kearns, Collins and Neuwelt*, 2003, (B).

3 Read through the introduction and get students to underline the key word in the example (iv) (*aim*). Then ask them to find matching information in paragraph A (*The main goal is to* …). Tell them to underline key words in the remaining questions, and set a time limit for the task to discourage reading in depth. Let students compare answers before checking, and ask them to justify their answers by reference to the text. It's worth pointing out that identifying the main topic in a paragraph is a key exam skill because it enables you to find relevant information quickly without reading the whole text.

4 Once students have read through the instructions, ask which reading skills they are likely to use (scanning). When checking, again ask students to justify their answers by identifying matching expressions in questions and text (see Key).

5 Read through the *Exam Briefing* and then study the definitions of True, False and Not Given answers in question 5. Discuss each one in more detail. With **True** statements, there is matching information in the text, though this will often be expressed in different words; With **False** statements, the information in the text says the opposite (= *contradicts*); **Not Given** statements contain information which is not mentioned in the text at all, even if it seems likely to be true.

NB There is more advice on choosing between No/False and Not Given statements on page 72.

Let students read through the instructions and *Task Approach*. With weaker students, you could give more support by asking them to jot down the paragraph references where relevant information for each question can be found. Check these as an interim stage, which will reinforce the *Task Approach*. When checking, ask students to justify their answers by referring to specific information in the text.

6 When checking, point out that although the article mentions the other points, they are not the main subject of the article. This is an important phase which can yield a lot of useful discussion. It encourages students to reflect on the task strategies they have used and to build the habit of cooperating and learning from other students. Spend time checking answers in detail, even if students have got most right. Ensure that they can justify their answers by reference to the text.

Focus on vocabulary *Dealing with unknown vocabulary (p.15)*

These exercises assume that students are familiar with the main parts of speech: *noun, verb, adjective,* and *adverb*. If not, it's important to introduce these terms now, because they represent a basic tool in preparing for IELTS and will be relevant to various tasks throughout this book. See *Key Language* Exercise 1.

1/2 Read through the introduction and then check briefly, e.g. *How do you know if a word is important to understand or not? What can help you guess the meaning of a word.* Then work through exercise 2 as a class.

3 Students can work individually or in pairs to complete the exercise but make sure they refer back to the text to study each expression in context. When checking, ask students to mention the clues which helped them answer, and draw their attention to any they have overlooked. In question 1, point out that *decline* is used as a noun in this context but that it can also be used as a verb, e.g. *Car sales have declined this year.* Explain that many words have more than one dictionary definition and only studying the context will determine which is correct.

KEY LANGUAGE

- **Grammatical terms**
  Exercise 1, page 210

Unit 1 Key

Lead-in (p.8)
See Student's Book, page 253.
1 C 2 E 3 A 4 D 5 B

Focus on reading 1 (p.9)
1 1 C 2 B 3 D 4 A
2 1 D 2 B, C 3 A 4 B
3 1 C (5 words *Quite simply …*)
  2 D (4 words *With Leapfrog …*)
  3 B (*was conducted, were observed*)
  4 A
  5 D (*Have you ever wished …?*)
  6 B (e.g. *conducted* = carried out, *adolescents* = teenagers/young people, *sedentary* = sitting, *observed* = noticed)
4 1 formal
  2 avoids
  3 impersonal
  4 few
  5 frequent
  6 precisely

Focus on speaking 2 (p.11)
2 1 both
  2 But/On the other hand
  3 main
  4 while/whereas
  5 Also/Another thing is that
  6 than

Focus on reading 2 (p.12)
2 3
3 1 iv (example)
  2 vi (use of present simple to describe routine)
  3 ii (*originated, spread, was adopted, continued to grow*)
  4 v (*health benefits, regular physical exercise,* etc.)
  5 iii (*socialise/talk to/chat*)
  6 i (*improves the quality of the urban environment, reducing congestion and pollution,* etc.)
  7 vii (*positive school image in the local community,* etc.)
4 1 A conductor (back = *rear* para B)
  2 1998 (did … begin = *originated* C)
  3 The United States (young children = *children aged 2 to 6* D)
5 1 TRUE (*there has been a significant decline in the number …* para A)
  2 FALSE (*regardless of the weather* B)
  3 FALSE (*the … concept originated in …England* C)
  4 NOT GIVEN (although this seems likely to be true there is no information about this in the passage)
  5 TRUE (*was adopted quickly in Australia … C*)
6 B

Focus on vocabulary (p.15)
2 adjective; large
3 a) noun, decrease
  b) verb, change
  c) noun, aim
  d) noun, advantage
  e) adjective, particular
  f) adverb, roughly
  g) noun, topic
  h) adjective, good or useful

2 ▶ Food for thought

To set the ball rolling ...

Begin by introducing the general topic of diet and eating habits. You could discuss typical breakfasts in different countries, the more varied the better, e.g. *full English breakfast* (fried egg, bacon, sausage, tomato and fried bread) or Japanese *natto* (fermented soya beans). If time allows, you could also design a small quiz where students match breakfast to country (see websites such as www.breakfastandbrunch.com/countryhome.php). Use the discussion to explore students' knowledge of and interest in the topic, and to introduce useful vocabulary. If the subject of healthy versus unhealthy eating comes up, keep this brief to avoid pre-empting the *Lead-in* discussion.

Lead-in *(p.18)*

Before students look at the table, ask them the question *Who eats more healthily, men or women?* Take a straw poll of their views and make a note of the result.

1 Once students have looked through the table, check any unfamiliar vocabulary, e.g. *skimmed (milk), fibre, cereal, wholemeal (bread), confectionery*. You could help by telling them there are five healthy and five unhealthy habits. Make sure they discuss ideas with their partner, rather than working alone. Ask a few pairs to report on their decisions and reasons, before they check the answers on page 253.

2 Focus on the *Why?* part of the question, encouraging students to formulate a satisfactory answer. If necessary, prompt them with: *Women tend to eat more ... and consume less ...* . Point out the usefulness of qualifying expressions like *generally* and *tend to*.

Focus on writing 1 *Interpreting data (p.19)*

NB Since decisions about tenses are relevant in many writing tasks, it's important that students are familiar with the main tenses. If they are at all hazy in this area, refer them to the reference list of tenses in the *Key Language Bank*, page 211. You may also wish to go through the accompanying exercise in class or set it for homework.

Read through the *Exam Briefing* as a class and discuss any questions students have.

1 Give students time to read the paragraphs and study the graphs, and then let them compare answers and ideas. After checking their answers, ask what they think the two vertical scales represent (A: grams per person per week; B: percentages). Then read through the two paragraphs again, highlighting each key expression. Focus on the word trend and point out that identifying overall trends is one of the most important aspects of interpreting graphs.

2 Read through the expressions in the *Useful language* box, checking understanding as necessary, before students do the task.

3 Monitor students' work and, after checking, focus on the organisation of the text, looking at how different components of the graph are linked (coherence).

If they are having problems, give extra practice with these or other graphs before doing exercise 4. This could be in the form of *Give me a sentence about the graph using the expression 'reached a peak'*, for example.

4 This is suitable for class or homework.

NB There is further practice of relevant language for describing data in *Key Language* Exercises 3 and 4 (see details below). These could be done in class or for homework.

KEY LANGUAGE

- **Names of tenses**
  Exercise 2, page 211
- **Adjectives describing change**
  Exercise 3, page 212
- **Reporting tenses**
  Exercise 4, page 212

Focus on speaking *Eating habits (p.21)*

1 This is another opportunity to check how aware of tenses and grammatical terms students are. Again encourage them to use the reference list of tenses in the *Key Language Bank*, page 211 if necessary. There is more information about the use of *-ing* forms after certain verbs and also about conditionals in *Key Language*, Exercises 15 and 27 (pages 221 and 229 respectively) but it is probably best to leave detailed study of these points till later in the course.

When checking answers, invite a few suggestions for suitable endings and explain they don't need to stick to the food/eating theme exclusively. Draw their attention to key language patterns. Give controlled practice if necessary to build fluency before students begin pairwork. Afterwards, invite a few pairs to report back on what their partner told them.

2 These are typical questions that might be asked in Part 1 of the Speaking Test. Point out that answers should be as full as possible and monitor students' discussions carefully, giving appropriate feedback afterwards.

Focus on listening 1 *Students' Union survey (p.22)*

Students may be alarmed at the idea of only hearing the recording once in the exam; training needs to strike a balance between developing listening skills and confidence, and accustoming students to the once-only format. For the first few tasks, you could play the recording again on request. Later on, you could read out problematic sections of the recording script for clarification and as a support to weaker students.

NB The recording is in two sections and, unless your students are very able, you may prefer to prepare for, and possibly check, each section separately.

Read through the *Exam Briefing* and give students a few minutes to study the instructions and questions 1–7. It's also a good idea to ask a few check questions, e.g. *What's the survey about? How do you mark the correct answer? Are all the questions of the same type? How many words can you use to answer the last three questions?* You could also let them discuss the food illustrated in questions 2 and 3.

Allow time for students to compare answers before the checking phase. Afterwards, you could focus on a few useful or interesting expressions, e.g. *I've never been (that) keen on …, once in a blue moon, to skip (breakfast), to have a sweet tooth.*

NB If students have difficulties with the spelling in question 8, it's worth giving further practice, e.g. British or Australian place names: *Leicester, Swansea, Bathurst, Kalgoorlie,* since this is a fairly regular feature of the exam.

Focus on listening 2 *Healthy eating (p.23)*

Allow plenty of time for the pre-listening phase. It's important that students guess answers in advance because this encourages the prediction strategy. In addition, by checking their answers when they listen, students will be practising the skills for a slightly different note completion task. (There is an example in Unit 4.)

Read through the *Exam Briefing,* the *Task Approach* and the task instructions.

Before students work together to guess answers, you could look at the first two questions and focus on the kind of word or expression that is needed. (question 1:

adjective modifying noun, e.g. *good, healthy*; question 2: either a general adverb like *much* or a more specific comparison like *three times*). Emphasise that it is the thinking which is important, not guessing the right answer. Even making a wild guess will make the listening process easier.

Before playing the recording, check that students have filled in all the spaces in pencil. You could also check a few predictions, especially for question 9, and deal with any unknown vocabulary, e.g. *poultry.*

Again, allow time for comparing answers before the checking phase. As a possible follow-up, you might want to focus on the difference between the two comparisons heard: *twice/three times as much* versus *ten/twenty times more.* NB See also *Key Language* Exercise 7, page 214.

Focus on writing 2 *Paragraphing (p.24)*

Remind students of the basic information about the Writing test in the *Exam Briefing* on page 19 if necessary.

1 Inappropriate paragraphing, or a failure to paragraph at all, is a common weakness in IELTS written work for Task 2. This introductory task is intended to underline the importance of paragraphing in communicating clearly to the reader. Discussions should cover both **when** to begin a new paragraph (with each main new idea) and **how** to do this clearly (indent or miss a line). Point out, if necessary, that paragraphing is highly relevant to Task 2 of the Writing module, but that it may be unnecessary to divide Task 1 answers into paragraphs when they are shorter and deal with a single topic.

2 Cohesion is a major factor in good writing, and this topic will recur later in the book. Ask students to study the two paragraphs and elicit ideas. In discussion, introduce the terms **grammatical** link, e.g. *which* and **logical** link, e.g. *but.* Then let them look through the reference list(s) in detail. You could point out that there is a fuller list of reference links in the *Key Language Bank,* page 217, but it's probably best to leave the exercises there till a later stage.

3/4/5 Give students time to work on the tasks alone and then compare answers. There are, of course, several acceptable ways of rewriting the text in exercise 5.

6 This is a useful revision task for students to work on in pairs. Make sure they check answers by reference to the *Useful language* and *Error Hit List,* and encourage them to add extra errors from their own written work for this unit. Check that the corrections are accurate!

Unit 2 Key

Lead-in (p.18)

1. See Student's Book, page 253.

2 Women generally have healthier diets than men because they tend to eat more fruit and vegetables on a daily basis, and they consume less sugar and fat.

Focus on writing 1 (p.19)

1

Graph	Paragraph	Activity
A	2	consumption of fruit and vegetables
B	1	cigarette smoking

2 b 1 a slight rise (in)
2 between 2000 and 2003; during the period 2000 to 2003
3 a sharp/steep/rapid decrease/fall (in)
4 to increase rapidly
5 to be at/reach a peak
6 to level out

3 1 a significant decline **2** (corresponding) rise
3 reached a peak **4** a steady/marked decline/fall
5 exceeded **6** a marked fall/decline **7** in about 1984 **8** a steady/significant increase/rise **9** 1994

4 (*Example answer*)
Of the various methods of payment which don't involve cash, cheques were the most popular **at the beginning of the period**. After that there was **a gradual decline** in the use of cheques, from approximately 2.3 billion in 1991 to just under 1 billion in 2007.

Credit and charge cards were the second most common non-cash method of payment in 1991 and their use **increased steadily for** about fourteen years before **levelling out** at about 1.8 billion.

There was a **steep rise** in debit card transactions **over the period**. These totalled less than 1 billion in 1991, but **increased rapidly** to 5 billion by 2007, making debit cards by far the most popular non-cash method of payment at that point.

Focus on speaking (p.21)

1 1 a) present simple
b) past simple
c) present simple; *enjoy/like/prefer + -ing*
d) present perfect (simple/continuous)
e) second conditional
f) past simple
g) present simple; *in* + noun or *-ing* form
h) (present simple +) present continuous/future simple

2 (*Example questions*)
a) What do you usually eat for breakfast?
b) When did you last have a meal in a restaurant?
c) Do you enjoy cooking?
d) How long have you been learning English?
e) Where would you go if you could choose any country in the world?
f) How long ago did you leave school?
g) How interested are you in politics/joining the swimming club?
h) When you finish your studies, what are you planning to do/will you do?

Focus on listening 1 (p.22)

1 B **2** C **3** B **4** C **5** C **6** B **7** A
8 Buckingham **9** Travel and Tourism
10 Second/2nd

Focus on listening 2 (p.23)

1 balanced **2** twenty (20) times **3** five (5)
4 carbonated **5** dairy products **6** three or four (3/4) **7** salt **8** three times a/per **9** avocado (pear) **10** twice as much

Focus on writing 2 (p.24)

1 a New paragraphs should begin at: *The reason people put on weight … Surveys show that …*
b 1 When writing about a subject where there are several aspects to be considered, for example an argument, a report or a detailed description; to enable the writer to organise his/her ideas clearly and to make it easier for the reader to follow them.
2 When you want to introduce a main new idea or topic.

2 Paragraph A is unnecessarily repetitive, and it is not clear which of the three sentences contains the main idea. By comparison, in paragraph B the three sentences have been linked together grammatically (*which*) and logically (*but*), making it easy to identify the main idea.

3 **A** although; Moreover
B Because; To; When

4 **C** (Before) that; such (societies); These (communities); those (prevailing); They
D the (meat eaten); that (found); which

5 (*Example answers*)
A We know that pizzas were eaten in ancient Pompeii, since brick pizza ovens have been uncovered there by archaeologists. However, early pizzas would have lacked one of their main modern ingredients because the first tomato seeds were not brought to Europe from Peru until 1,500 years later.

> **B** Although tomatoes were held in low esteem by most Europeans, the poor people of Naples added them to their yeast dough and created the first modern pizza. By the 17th century, pizza was popular with visitors, who would go to poor neighbourhoods to taste the peasant dish, (which was) made by men called *pizzaioli*.
>
> **6** UL = *Useful Language* p.21; EHL = *Error Hit List* p.26
>
> 1 *Example* (UL)
> 2 which ~~they~~ were out of date … (EHL)
> 3 an increase <u>in</u> expenditure. (EHL)
> 4 <u>fell</u> last year. (EHL)
> 5 <u>for</u> ten years. (UL)
> 6 have <u>increased/risen</u> (EHL)
> 7 go ~~for~~ swimming (EHL)
> 8 a <u>slight</u> decrease (UL)

Reflective Learning 1 *(p.27)*

Useful vocabulary: reflect (on), reflective, goal, monitor, factor, consolidate

Motivation is everything, so it's essential that students are completely clear about the point of these sections and that they see them as interesting and relevant to their studies.

For that reason, it's worth spending time on this introductory section in order to underline the importance of reflective learning, not only in preparing for IELTS as effectively as possible, but also as the basis for their future academic study. (See main *Introduction* page 6.)

1 Read through the introduction here together and clarify the terms *reflect (on)* (= think carefully about) and *reflective* (= thoughtful). When students have completed the task and checked answers on page 258, discuss the issues in more detail.

Additional notes:

- A mistake can only be productive if you take time to reflect on it and establish exactly what went wrong. This may be a simple matter or it may mean revisiting a more complex area of grammar, but in that way it should be possible to eliminate the mistake in future.

- The need to accept ambiguity and uncertainty is inevitable in academic study but is also relevant to IELTS, where you may need to rely on your 'best guess' as to the meaning of a word in a reading or listening text.

2 Give students time to read through all three sections and make brief notes, then let them discuss experiences in pairs.

Afterwards open a class discussion. Point out that we all tend to develop rigid ideas about the right way to do things, based on what we've experienced in the past, and that this can be a handicap to successful study. It's essential to keep an open mind and be ready to experiment with any new approaches that can assist learning.

3 Let the scores students award themselves remain private, but do monitor the learning goals they list and stress the importance of follow-through. Encourage them to keep a record of learning, and to make a point of reviewing goals regularly. The **Plan/Do/Review** cycle could be recorded in the form of a little chart. You could give an example layout with one line completed as an example.

Key: See Student's Book, page 258.

3 ▶ Location is everything

To set the ball rolling ...

Introduce the topic of cities and urban living briefly with books closed. You could ask students to name the odd one out from a list of cities on the board, e.g. *Paris, New York, Bangkok, Cairo, London, Buenos Aires* (odd one out = New York – not a capital city). Follow up with a few general questions, e.g. *Have you visited any of these cities? Which city would you most like to visit? Is it better to live in a city than in the country? Why/Why not?*

Lead-in *(p.28)*

1 This is a short activity for pair discussion, which touches on some of the topics in the unit. Students can check the answers on page 253. NB These are also included in the Key on page 18, which contains some additional facts and figures.

2 Let students read through the descriptions individually and then discuss ideas in pairs. If they need help, tell them they can choose from the list of cities in question 1, and if they are still struggling, you could supply the following extra clues:

> **A** It is sometimes known as the 'Paris of the East'. The country it's in has one of the fastest growing economies in the world.
> **B** The city originally began life as a prison settlement. The Olympic Games were held there in 2000.
> **C** One of its suburbs is associated with the film industry.
> **D** The city is well below sea level and most of the country it belongs to has been reclaimed from the sea.

Let students check answers on page 253. NB These are also included in the Key on page 18, which contains some additional facts and figures. Discuss answers and highlight any interesting/useful expressions, e.g. **A** *cargo, historic (vs historical)*, **B** *landmark,* **C** *(be) devoted to,* **D** *bicycle-friendly, the Stock Exchange*

3 Students could create their own city descriptions for others to guess, if time allows.

NB *Key Language* Exercise 5 revises the form and use of the passive voice. It would be useful to include this exercise in order to highlight the importance of the passive in academic writing.

KEY LANGUAGE

- **The passive**
  Exercise 5, page 212
  Suggested approach for classwork
- Write the example active sentence on the board and check that students can identify the *subject* and *object*. Elicit the passive version and write it up.
- Check the term *agent*, and introduce the terms *long* and *short passive*. Ask which is more common, and what kind of writing they would expect to find most examples of the short passive in. Students can check answers in the *Language fact* box on page 213.
- If you feel your students would benefit from a more detailed analysis of the form, you could look at the various tenses possible and also the use of the infinitive, with and without *to*, e.g. *He asked to be excused. The problem could be solved.*

Focus on speaking 1 *Urban problems (p.29)*

1/2 It's worth pointing out that urban problems, such as population growth, are a very common IELTS topic. Let students check answers to exercise 2 on page 253 before they move on to the next exercise.

3 When students have completed task **a**, check answers and clarify vocabulary as necessary. Introduce task b giving a few examples to show how several combinations are possible. Encourage students to include vocabulary from exercise 3.

4 If mindplans are new to students, it's best to work through the initial stages as a class. Ask students to suggest more headings, e.g. *Population, Pollution*, and to add examples. It's important not to be too prescriptive, nor to complete the task at this stage. Point out that there isn't one 'right answer', and that each mindplan will reflect an individual way of thinking.

Focus on reading *Location is everything (p.30)*

1 Ask students to cover the text before eliciting answers to exercise 1a. Then give them a minute or so to skim the text. Check answers carefully to make sure they have a real overview (i.e. an idea of the whole text, rather than only one aspect of it).

2 Let students compare ideas before checking answers.

3 Read through the *Exam Briefing* and *Task Approach*. Encourage students to write on the reading text and point out that they can and should write on the exam paper, which may surprise them.

Ask students to highlight the cities **A–I** in the text. (Make sure they don't include other place names.) The text doesn't always specify which country a city is in, and although it's not actually necessary to know this, being able to 'place' a city is probably helpful in terms of confidence. So, if your students' general knowledge is shaky, you may want to check that they know where one or two cities are, and also the modern name for Constantinople (Istanbul).

Focus on the example and ask students to find the relevant parallel expressions in the text (grew into a successful trading city = *was prospering thanks to trade*; location close to the sea = *proximity to the sea*). It may be helpful to repeat this procedure for the first question, as a class.

Let students compare answers, and when checking, make sure they can justify their answers by reference to the text. You may need to clarify one or two vocabulary items, e.g. *swamp* (question 4) and *periphery* (question 6).

4/5/6 Sentence completion is quite a challenging task type, and this introduction will probably need to be paced quite slowly, with time to complete the introductory tasks, and plenty of support in tackling the task itself.

Read through the *Exam Briefing* and *Task Approach* and then ask students to complete exercises 5 and 6 and compare answers before checking.

7 Read through the instructions and example. It would help to do question 9 as a class. Ask students to think of another word for *farming* and elicit *agriculture*. Tell them to find where this word first appears (line 7) and read the information carefully, before choosing the best ending. Check that they can justify the answer (I) *live permanently in one place* = settle down and live …

It's important that students use their reading skills rather than their guessing skills to complete the task! Monitor to make sure they are reading the text carefully.

Let students compare answers and check they can identify the relevant parallel phrases in the text.

Focus on speaking 2 *Describing places (p.34)*

Remind students about the format of the Speaking test and read through the *Exam Briefing*.

1 Monitor the pair work and ask one or two students to report back on what their partner said.

2 Make sure students realise they have to refer to the maps to complete the text. Afterwards, check vocabulary as necessary, e.g. *in* the west vs **to** the west; *attractions* vs *amenities*.

3 Give students a general idea of what happens in Part 2 of the Speaking test, which is called the 'Long turn' (this is described in detail in the *Exam Briefing* box on page 61). Point out that in order to keep talking for 1–2 minutes, they will need to mention several aspects of a subject. Explain that they will be able to make notes beforehand and remind them about mindplans (page 30), which are a useful way of doing this.

4 Where there are two (or more) students of the same nationality, they can usefully work together in pairs or small groups to make notes. However, students should swap groups/pairs before giving their descriptions. Monitor carefully, noting key areas for attention. For additional speaking practice, students could use the same headings to compare their own cities, or to compare their city with the place they will be studying at (ask the question *What differences do you expect?*).

NB There is a *Key Language* exercise on describing geographical positions (see below). This should be a fairly quick revision, but it's an important area and there are some points which are well worth clarifying.

5 This is a good task for pairwork. Remind students that mistakes are an opportunity for learning, not a sign of failure. Make sure they do the exercise before referring to the *Error Hit List* on page 46. Check that corrections are accurate, and encourage students to add extra errors from their own written work for this unit.

KEY LANGUAGE

- **Geographical positions**
  Exercise 6, page 213
  Suggested approach for classwork
- Let students work in pairs to read and discuss questions 1–4. When checking, add further examples to clarify, as necessary.
- For question 5, students should work individually before checking answers in pairs. With weaker students, it may be worth getting them to write out their answers, and checking their use of capitals carefully.
- Use the other places marked for extra oral or written practice as necessary.

Unit 3 Key

Lead-in *(p.28)*

1 NB These answers are given in the Student's Book (p.253), but more detail is included here.

1 Tokyo (35.3 million), (=2. Mexico City, New York, 4. São Paolo, 5. Mumbai)
2 Rome (c. 1 million)
3 Singapore
4 Mexico City (2,255m above sea level)
5 Bangkok. Although other cities such as Dubai may be hotter at certain times, Bangkok maintains an average temperature above 30°C day and night, all year round.
6 Hong Kong is well ahead of New York City (2) and São Paulo (3) (For details, see Emporis.com)

2 NB These answers are given in the Student's Book (p. 253), but more detail is included here.

A Shanghai, China
B Sydney, Australia (400 settlers and 750 convicts arrived from Britain in 1788 to develop the area as a penal colony)
C Los Angeles, USA (the centre of the film industry is, of course, Hollywood)
D Amsterdam, Netherlands (If sea levels rise, it will be one of the first cities to be flooded.)

Focus on speaking 1 *(p.29)*

1 (environmental) pollution

1 The large number of cars (and also the geographical situation of Los Angeles, surrounded by hills).
2 (*Example answer*)
Because pollution can cause serious health problems and also contributes to global warming.
3 (*Example answers*)
Fuel could be taxed more heavily; public transport could be improved; alternative 'greener' forms of fuel should be developed.

2 See Student's Book, page 253.

3 a (*Example answers*) **Work:** child labour, unemployment, working conditions
Healthcare: drugs, hospital equipment, medical staff,
Education: teachers, textbooks, truancy
Housing (problems): homelessness, overcrowding, slums
Environment (*-al* problems): greenhouse gases, pollution, toxic waste

b (*Example answers*) NB many permutations are possible
insufficient prescription drugs
inadequate hospital equipment
inappropriate textbooks
poor working conditions
serious unemployment
severe overcrowding
damaging greenhouse gases
growing/increasing homelessness
trained/qualified teachers

4 (*Example answers*)
Crime: e.g. drug-related crime, young offenders, growing prison population
Population: e.g. migration to cities, population explosion
Employment: e.g. inadequate employment opportunities
Transport: e.g. serious traffic congestion, damaging pollution
Housing/Living conditions: homelessness, poor housing, lack of basic services (gas/electricity/water)
Healthcare: e.g. need for sufficient trained doctors/nurses, hospital equipment, prescription drugs
Education: e.g. need for sufficient trained teachers, books, school equipment
Other: e.g. care of the elderly, environmental awareness

Focus on reading *(p.30)*

1 a (*Example answer*)
The importance of location in the development of the world's major cities.

2 2

3 1 C *banking came to dominate its economy* (lines 67–68)
2 I *By the 1930s … New York … world's first city with a population of ten million* (111–116)
3 B *became rich by weaving wool* (65)
4 F *founded … on swamp land* (90)
5 D *largest city and premiere trading centre* (70–71)
6 H *stations are dotted around the periphery* (instead of located centrally) (106–107)
7 A *the city's power went into steep decline* (32–33)
8 G *Thousands of slave labourers died during its construction* (98–99)

5 1 citizens, inhabitants   2 depended on, couldn't manage without   3 followed, came afterwards   4 leaving, abandoning   5 migrating back, returning   6 started developing, appeared   7 easy to reach, convenient to get to   8 ridiculously, foolishly   9 huge, enormous

6 1 9, 11, 13   2 10, 12, 14

7 *Example*: not so many = *fewer*; were required = *were needed*

9 I farming = *agriculture*; live permanently in one place (I) = *settle down and live*
   10 C protection (C) = *defence*
   11 G began to grow and prosper = *flourished*; made money (G) = *became wealthier*
   12 D lost its power = *went into steep decline*; its dependence on (D) = *became reliant on*
   13 A established = *founded*; convenient (A) = *accessible*
   14 E religious (E) = *sacred*

Focus on speaking 2 *(p.34)*

2 1 (situated) in the west   2 population   3 is (situated) on/lies on   4 includes   5 called   6 in/near the   7 (to the) north-west   8 (tourist) attractions   9 amenities

5 1 … a large/considerable/substantial amount …
   2 A number of cities have …
   3 ✓
   4 … have a high level …
   5 A number of surveys have been …
   6 Only a small percentage of the houses have …
   7 ✓
   8 … a higher standard of living.
   9 … is not in proportion to the size …
   10 Compared with …

4 ▶ Haves and have-nots

To set the ball rolling …

As this unit develops a topic area related to Unit 3, there is no need for a separate introduction. However, you could take a few minutes to revise useful topic vocabulary from the previous unit, e.g. *megacity, accessible, amenities*, together with language points from the *Spot the Error* task on page 25.

Lead-in *(p.38)*

1 This introduction is an opportunity to highlight some topic areas and to check some key topic vocabulary. NB the figure for 2013 is a UN estimate.

2 Although students are unlikely to know the answers to this quiz, encourage them to discuss the questions in pairs and to make intelligent guesses. Make sure that they have marked their chosen answers before checking answers on page 253. NB The Key on page 22 includes some interesting comparative figures which are not in the Student's Book, and which you can feed into the checking phase as appropriate.

Explain that the results for question 5 are based on *The Human Development Index* (HDI) published annually by the UN. This aims to measure three dimensions of human development: living a long and healthy life, being educated and having a decent standard of living. The criteria used for measuring these are listed in the answer to exercise 1, question 3 in the Key on page 22. For more information see http://hdr.undp.org/en/statistics

Once students have checked answers, invite them to express a personal reaction by asking if any of the results surprised or shocked them – you could usefully introduce the phrases *I didn't realise that …, It's really … that …* here (see *Useful language* on page 148). It's best not to discuss the answers further at this point to avoid duplicating the discussion points in the *Focus on speaking* section which follows.

Focus on speaking *Standards of living (p.39)*

1 Point out that being able to express an opinion clearly and appropriately is fundamental to successful performance in the Speaking test. Ask students to study the *Useful language*, and make sure they know the mistakes to avoid.

2 Monitor the pair work and afterwards have a brief whole-class round-up of ideas. Identify one or two language points to focus on for remedial practice if appropriate.

Focus on writing 1 *Interpreting and comparing data (p.39)*

1 As an alternative to the procedure in the book, and for speed, you could read out the questions, inviting students to guess answers (without accepting or rejecting these). Move on quickly to the following task without letting students check answers!

2 This orientation task needs to be completed quickly if it's to develop key skimming/scanning skills, so set a tight time limit (say 1 minute). When checking answers, ask for key words from the diagrams, e.g. C *read and write* = literacy. Make sure students label the diagrams correctly before continuing.

3/4 Let students collaborate on these tasks if they want, and again set a time limit. Briefly check answers to exercise 4 in relation to previous guesses.

5 Monitor students' work and use this exercise for diagnostic purposes.

NB If you detect a general weakness in this area of comparatives, do *Key Language* Exercise 7 as a class, before moving on to exercise 6. Otherwise, set it for individual or class homework.

6 There is more scope for error here, so monitor carefully in order to steer weaker students in the right direction.

7 The information in the table is quite complex, in that units of measurement vary and high figures may be good, e.g. *clean air* or bad, e.g. *murders*. For this reason, it's worth spending time making sure that students are absolutely clear about the correct interpretations.

As an introduction, you could ask a few preliminary questions, e.g. (Los Angeles): *What does the figure 12.5 represent? And 12.4? Is that high or low?* (Noise): *Which is quietest: 1 or 10?* Explain if necessary that *ambient* means 'in the surrounding area'. Students might find it helpful to circle the best or worst figures in each area with different colours prior to discussion.

Include the writing phase **c** in class time if possible, so that students can exchange ideas and you can monitor their work. Use this task as a diagnostic tool to help you decide whether to do *Key Language* Exercise 8 on comparatives as a class, or recommend it to individuals. NB There are sample answers in the *Writing Practice Bank* with focus questions highlighting some key language features. This exercise can be done in class or for homework, but it's important to check answers thoroughly as a class.

KEY LANGUAGE

- **Numerical and other comparative expressions**
  Exercise 7, page 214
- **Forming comparatives and superlatives**
  Exercise 8, page 215

WRITING PRACTICE

- **Comparing data (example answer)** Exercise 1,
  page 235

Focus on listening 1 *Wasting energy (p.42)*

NB The recording is in two sections, and unless your students are very able, you may prefer to prepare for, and possibly check, each section separately.

In this case, read through the *Exam Briefing* and give students a few minutes to look at the *Task Approach*, and study the bar graph for questions 1 and 2.

At the end of the first section, pause the recording. You could also check answers at this stage. Give students time to read through questions 3–10 and invite some guesses as to possible answers.

After playing the recording, give students time to compare their answers. If necessary, replay the recording, section by section, as you check answers.

Focus on writing 2 *Paragraphing (p.44)*

Inappropriate paragraphing in exam written work can be as much of a problem as not paragraphing, and students need to be aware that paragraphs rarely consist of a single sentence. Before you begin, briefly revise the reasons for paragraphing discussed in Unit 2.

1/2/3/4 Check that students are quite clear about the terms *topic*, *supporting* and *qualifying*, and clarify further if necessary. Make sure there's an agreed order for the sentences in exercise 3 before they go on to exercise 4. Remind them of the linking expressions in Unit 2, and refer them back to the lists on pages 24 and 25 if necessary, before they begin.

5 Read through the *Exam Briefing* as a class and then let students study the exam topic. Point out that mindplans are a very useful way of organising your thoughts in preparation for writing (as well as speaking), and ask them to find the mindplan they drew up in Unit 3 (page 30).

Ask students to work in pairs to:

1 add new headings/ideas from the information in this unit, e.g. *Employment* and *Education*;

2 decide which two problems are the most important or urgent to tackle;

3 discuss possible strategies for tackling them.

Have a round-up of ideas before continuing (or combine pairs to swap ideas). The writing task could usefully be done in class if time allows, so that students can benefit from some immediate feedback. NB There is an example answer in the *Writing Practice Bank* (see below) with focus questions highlighting some key features of paragraphing. This exercise can be done in class or for homework but it's important to check answers thoroughly as a class.

WRITING PRACTICE

- **Presenting the solution to a problem (example answer)** Exercise 2, page 236

Focus on listening 2 *Case study: São Paulo (p.45)*

NB Again, you may prefer to prepare for each section of the recording separately. In this case, note that the *Task Approach* applies to questions 5–10, so it's best to delay studying this until students have completed the first section of the recording.

Tell students they're going to hear a lecture about the city of São Paolo in Brazil. Before playing the first section, you could also ask them to suggest any facts they know about Brazil. Then let them look through the instructions and questions 1–4. Remind them that they must follow the lecture and answer questions while they listen.

At the end of the first section, pause the recording. (You may wish to check answers at this stage.) Give students time to study the *Task Approach* for completing diagrams, then focus their attention on the layout: **main heading** (centre) and **subheadings** (arranged around), and also ask them to check which way the questions go: clockwise or anticlockwise.

Give them time to study the instructions and questions 5–10. Point out that, in the exam, they can write more than three words in the question booklet if necessary and then transfer the three key words to the answer sheet.

Let students compare answers before checking. You may want to replay the recording as you check answers, to clear up any misunderstandings, and also focus on useful expressions such as *shanty towns*, *settle in*, *stumbling block*.

Unit 4 Key

Lead-in (p.38)
1 (*Example answers and notes*)
  1 The very rapid (exponential) rate of increase in recent years.
  2 Clean water, living conditions (housing, sanitation, etc.), hygiene, diet, healthcare, immunisation + genes.
  3 Life expectancy, literacy, school enrolment, educational attainment, per capita GDP (these are the criteria used for analysing quality of life in the UN's *Human Development Index* (HDI). Other possible factors might include: air quality, crime figures, health and educational facilities, as well as more contentious issues like the position of women and freedom of expression.
2 See Student's Book, page 253.
  Additional notes for questions 5–8:
  5 The next highest ranking were Australia and Canada. The criteria for calculating rankings are listed in the Key for exercise 1, question 3 above.
  6 The figure represents the number enrolled as a percentage of the relevant age group. The next highest ranking countries were Finland and South Korea, each with 93%. Source: *The Economist.*
  7 The next highest ranking were Australia (81.6), and Canada (81.2). NB The world average is 66.6. Source: US Census Bureau.
  8 The next hardest working countries are the Czech Republic (1,986 hours), Poland (1,983) and Slovakia (1,958). Source: *Organisation for Economic Cooperation and Development.*

Focus on writing 1 (p.39)
1 **1** an Australian   **2** Europe   **3** Latvia
  4 country   **5** city
2 **1** B   **2** C   **3** D   **4** A
3 **1** numbers of years
  2 women; in Australia
  3 five; countries
  4 numbers of patients per doctor
  5 Latvia
  6 literacy levels in different continents
  7 Female, Male
  8 percentages (of the population)
  9 77% (25% + 52%)
 10 83% (46% + 37%)
5 **A** **1** identical   **2** twice   **3** the greatest
  B **4** twenty times
  C **5** much lower   **6** (very) little (NB *a marginal* is also possible)
  D **7** (exactly) a quarter   **8** almost half
6 (*Example answers*)
  1 Africa is the continent with the greatest difference in literacy rates between men and women. / In Africa the literacy rate for men is almost 50% **higher than** that for women.

2 Doctors in Nepal have 100/one hundred times **as many** patients **as** doctors in Latvia. / Doctors in Nepal have 100/one hundred times **more** patients **than** …
3 In 1990, 58% of the world's population lived in rural areas, but by 2025, this is expected to be **much lower**.
7 **a** **1** London   **2** Mexico City   **3** Mexico City
    4 Tokyo   **5** Los Angeles   **6** London and Tokyo
  c See example answers in *Writing Practice* Exercise 1, page 235.

Focus on listening 1 (p.42)
1 E   **2** A   **3** twenty (20) days   **4** damp   **5** 80
6 Plastics   **7** 4,000 years   **8** temperature
9 humidity   **10** oxygen

Focus on writing 2 (p.44)
1 **a** The influence of the car on the design of modern cities.
  b The first sentence = the topic statement. Supporting points = **1** high level of car ownership reflected in low-density layout of cities; **2** freeway systems designed to facilitate regular long-distance driving
2 The last sentence.
3 Topic statement 3
  Supporting point(s) 1
  Qualifying statement 5
  Supporting point(s) 2, 4
4 See example answer in *Writing Practice* Exercise 2, page 236

Focus on listening 2 (p.45)
1 1554
2 16.5 million
3 cars and computers
4 coffee trade
5 not enough/lack of money
6 Floods
7 variety of work
8 entertainment
9 (hospitals and) health
10 transport

Critical Thinking 1 (p.47)

Useful vocabulary: analyse/analysis/analytical, essential, effective, evaluate, distinguish (between), option

Critical Thinking is the final academic strand, and will probably be the least familiar to students. For that reason, it's worth spending time on this introductory section in order to establish exactly what critical thinking is (and isn't) and to make sure students are aware of its importance to the success of their studies. (See main *Introduction* page 6).

Read through the introduction here together and explain that the term has no negative connotations. 'Critical' here refers to a positive process, careful analytical thinking, rather than to finding faults in something.

1/2 Tell students that the thinking process is much more important than simply getting the 'right' answer. Point out that there may be several 'right' answers. Look at the example answers for exercise 2, and explain that others could be added, e.g. *golf* (because it's the only word with just only one syllable!).

Let students work in pairs. Monitor their discussions, encouraging them to be as creative as possible. When checking, emphasise the variety of valid answers that are possible.

NB Students can also design their own categorisation and/or spot the difference tasks for critical thinking practice and vocabulary revision. These may serve as useful filler activities.

3 This task calls for more creative thinking and can lead to a very productive discussion about the language learning process. You could go through the first as an example or just let students work things out for themselves.

Example answers:

Similarities: learning to drive involves practising certain skills repeatedly until they become automatic; you make lots of mistakes when you're a learner driver; you have to learn certain rules, etc.

Differences: you don't need any equipment to learn a language; you don't have to take a test before you can use the language 'in public'; children generally learn languages more easily than adults, etc.

4 Point out that little or no learning will take place with the brain switched off! Even activities which may appear 'mindless', such as copying or repeating, are only useful if there is some degree of mental engagement. However, several of the activities call for more complex mental processes (see Key), and it's best to focus on one or two of these first, before asking students to discuss the rest in pairs.

Then ask them to consider questions 3 and 7 and discuss what mental (and physical) processes are needed for these to be useful learning activities.

Example answers:

3 listening for understanding, comparing what you hear with what you already know about the sounds and vocabulary of English, using your knowledge of English sound/spelling relationships to guess the spelling of an unknown word, if necessary, etc.

7 noticing exact sounds and stress patterns, (watching the shape of teacher's mouth when producing the sounds), comparing the sounds you hear with other sounds you know, and noticing similarities and differences, being aware of your own vocal organs and the shape of your mouth as you speak, comparing the sound you make with the model you have heard, etc.

Key: See Student's Book, page 259.

5 ▶ Hurry Sickness

To set the ball rolling ...

The *Lead-in* provides a personal introduction to the unit but if you have time you could usefully begin by discussing the concept of 'Work-life balance', which should generate an interesting range of topic vocabulary. Ask if students can explain the term (first used in the 1970s, it describes the balance between an individual's work and personal life). Then discuss the following points:

- In recent years there has been a substantial increase in working hours (in America these have risen from 43 hours a week, to 47 in two decades). What could be the reason for this? e.g. the effects of information technology, the increasingly competitive work environment with its emphasis on performance and results, the consumer society, etc.
- What are the negative effects? e.g. stress and 'burnout' caused by overwork, resulting in health and interpersonal relationship problems.
- Who else is affected by this problem apart from the individual? e.g. families, employers through the decrease in productivity and the cost of sick leave and absenteeism, and ultimately the national economy.
- How can the problem be tackled? e.g. employers could impose a limit on the number of hours worked per week and make annual leave (= holiday) compulsory; they could also support flexible working hours, offer stress management programmes, etc.

NB You could develop this into a fuller speaking practice by asking students to work in pairs or small groups to prepare five tips on how to achieve a better work-life balance in their lives. They could then explain some or all of these to the class.

Lead-in *(p.48)*

1 The task is self-explanatory but make sure students work in pairs and actually discuss each question. Let them check the Key on page 253 and then ask them to report back briefly on their conversations. Clarify expressions like *get to the point, frustrated, irritable* if necessary.

2 Monitor students' discussions and check that they are expressing opinions appropriately (see *Useful language* page 39) and giving reasons. Let them report back before revealing the correct answers.

At that point you could ask if any results surprised them, and perhaps practise the phrases: *It's really interesting/surprising …, It's not really surprising that …, (I suppose) It's fairly predictable that …*

3/4 Give students a few minutes to read through the text, then ask them to cover it before answering questions 1–3 in pairs.

5 Let students compare answers and check meanings as necessary.

Focus on speaking 1 *Stereotypes (p.49)*

Clarify the term 'stereotype', perhaps asking students what the general opinion about people/the weather/the food in Britain is. Use the two patterns from the *Useful language* box (*supposed to be be/supposed to have*) to talk about these preconceptions. For further practice, discuss a few more countries, including perhaps, the students' own.

Ask students to work in pairs to do the exercises and monitor to make sure they're using the target language. Afterwards ask students to report back and have a brief discussion about stereotypes. Ask: *Why do they exist? How accurate are they? What are the dangers?*

Focus on reading 1 *Hurry sickness (p.49)*

1 a Help students explore ideas about the title: Is it a real illness? How does *hurry* relate to the idea of modern life? How is life different today from 100 years ago? etc.

b Set a time limit of 4 to 5 minutes for global reading (skimming) to prevent students getting bogged down by reading this quite dense text in detail. When checking, look also at why wrong answers are wrong and emphasise, as ever, the need to have a clear idea of the overall topic.

2 Check if students remember the term 'scanning' and ask them to check the definition on page 12 if necessary. Point out that being able to locate specific information in a long reading passage quickly is an essential skill for many exam questions.

3 Read through the *Exam Briefing* and *Task Approach*, and then work through the initial steps, as a class. Ask students to identify key words in the list of headings and to compare results. Give them time to read through Section A and ask them to say what it's about in their own words. They should compare ideas before checking the correct answer. Repeat for Section D. Ask if these headings summarise or pick out key information.

The exam task itself is intended to be fairly straightforward and confidence-building. When checking, ask students to justify their answers by reference to the text.

4/5 While students should be familiar with conventional multiple-choice questions (question 7), they may not have met the variation shown in questions 8–10, which is a common IELTS task-type. Read through the *Task Approach*, paying special attention to the three key questions. Point out that in questions like 8–10, answers can be given in any order, and stress the need to find evidence for the correct answers in the text.

6 Make sure students notice the key instruction: that answers must be words or phrases from the text. Remind them of the importance of scanning to find the relevant section before reading for detail. If students are struggling, you can help by giving them paragraph references, e.g. question 11 (para B), question 12 (para C), etc.

7 This exercise encourages self-help skills in dealing with vocabulary in reading texts. Before beginning, remind students about the guidelines for dealing with unknown vocabulary (page 15). While checking, clarify further as necessary.

NB Affixes are also a useful clue to working out the meaning of words, and there are *Key Language* exercises in this area of language (see below). These exercises can be completed in class or set for homework, as appropriate.

KEY LANGUAGE

- **Word building: Affixes**
  Exercise 9, page 216
  Suggested approach for classwork
- Introduce the terms *affix*, *prefix* and *suffix* with examples on the board and then let students work through the four tasks.
- Further concept checking and/or clarification may be necessary.
- Set a task requiring students to use some of this vocabulary.

Focus on reading 2 *Distinguishing fact from opinion (p.55)*

This is a brief introduction to an important reading skill, which is required for a range of IELTS reading questions. The aim is to raise students' awareness of the kind of verbal clues which suggest that the writer is expressing a subjective opinion. Let students compare answers and discuss as necessary.

Focus on speaking 2 *Priorities (p.55)*

As an alternative approach, students could work in pairs to try and reach agreement on their lists. Either way, monitor pair work to ensure that the topics are being discussed in reasonable depth and also to note any language areas which need attention. Finish with a round-up of opinions and feedback, as necessary.

NB These are suitable issues for Task 2 writing topics, too.

Unit 5 Key

Lead-in (p.48)

2 See Student's Book page 253. **Additional notes:**
The ranking for each city (out of 32) is shown in
brackets. Singapore (1), Madrid (3), Guanzhou
(4), New York (8), Wellington (15) Cairo (24)

4 (*Example answers*)
1 They have become (about 10 per cent) faster.
(para 1)
2 Because they are a sign of the pace of people's
lives (para 2)
3 People who walk fast are less helpful to other
people and are more likely to suffer from heart
disease. (paras 3/4)

5 The numbers in brackets show which *Academic
Vocabulary* sections these items are practised in.
1 conducted (AV 1)
2 revealed (AV 1)
3 significant (AV 1, 2, 3, 9, 10)
4 indicator (AV 7 indicate)
5 previous (AV 1, 7)
6 linked (AV 6)

Focus on reading 1 (p.49)

1 b C

2 1 stress-related illness
2 nearly 40 years
3 a sociologist

3 v (example)
1 vii
2 ix
i (example)
3 iii
4 vi
5 x
6 ii

4 7 B *people pull their cell phones out* … (section D)
8–10 (in any order)
B *human beings are not designed* … (E)
D *there is increased pressure to do more* … (C)
E *In the past, an overnight letter* … (C)
G *Because the technology is available to us,* … (C)

5 Results of hurry sickness rather than causes: C, F
Factors not mentioned in the text: A, G

6 11 degree and intensity (B)   12 technology (C)
13 (physical) health (E)   14 become aware of (H)

7 1 (verb) h)
2 (noun) e)
3 (noun) a)
4 (verb) c)
5 (plural noun) f)
6 (adjective) g)
7 (noun) b)
8 (adjective) d)

Focus on reading 2 (p.55)

1 1 On my way to work once, … razor (F); which
seemed to me extraordinary. (O)
2 James Gleick is a science writer and the author
of several books … (F) … fascinating … (O)
3 F
4 … the undoubted speed of the internet (F),
there's a sense … impatient (O)

2 1 O   6 F
2 F   7 O
3 O   8 O
4 F   9 O
5 O   10 F

6 ▶ Time out

To set the ball rolling ...

Ask students to guess which leisure activities are most popular in the UK. (Walking is by far the most popular physical activity/sport, while watching TV is the most popular home-based activity.) You could also mention that DIY, gardening and driving for pleasure are top-ten pastimes. Then briefly discuss this in relation to popular leisure activities in students' countries.

Lead-in (p.58)

1 Check instructions for Part a and ask students to complete the task individually first. Before the pair discussion (b), you could demonstrate a variety of questions that can be used by asking one or two students about one of their chosen activities. Monitor students' conversations and note any errors to deal with, as necessary.

Afterwards get students to report back briefly on what they've discovered about their partner's leisure activities. You could go on to incorporate more targeted language practice, if appropriate, e.g. *I spend much less time reading than X does.*

2 a Let students work in pairs to discuss these questions, and have a brief round-up of ideas afterwards. If necessary, remind them of language for giving opinions (page 39).

b The tables of results on page 237 provide a good basis for a class discussion. If you have a mixed sex class, it may be interesting to compare male/female results for the class with those from the official survey.

The tables also provide practice of comparisons (see *Key Language Bank* Exercises 7 and 8, pages 214/215), which can lead on to the guided writing activity on the same page.

Writing Practice Exercise 4, page 238 also provides a model Task 1 answer with focus questions, which is suitable for classwork or homework.

WRITING PRACTICE

- **Presenting and comparing data (guided practice)**
  Exercise 3, page 237
  Suggested approach for classwork
  Oral practice: Ask students to work through questions 1–6 in exercise 1 and check answers. In pairs or as a class they should describe two main similarities between the tables and two significant differences, e.g. *Watching TV is the most popular leisure activity for both men and women. Reading is much more popular with women than men. Around 75 per cent of women enjoy reading compared with only 55 per cent of men.*
  NB If students need to revise the language of comparison, refer them to Exercises 7 and 8 in the *Key Language Bank* (pages 214 and 215).
  Writing practice: Exercise 2 can be completed in class or set for homework. When checking, draw students' attention to linking expressions like *However*, and to the opening and closing sentences.
- **Presenting and comparing data (example answer)**
  Exercise 4, page 238

Focus on vocabulary *Describing people (p59)*

1 This activity is best done with books closed so that students are not distracted by the lists of adjectives. Write the five people on the board and check understanding if necessary (a *kayak* is a kind of canoe, in which the place where you sit is covered over).

2 Students can work alone or in pairs. Explain any unknown vocabulary, e.g. *cerebral, introspective.* When checking, ask them to single out the attributes which helped them identify each activity.

3 This activity can be done in pairs, or for speed, as a class. Point out they can use any adjectives, not only those on the lists.

> **Optional activity**
> Ask students to write four to five adjectives on a piece of paper to describe someone who enjoys their favourite activity. Collect students' lists (with names for identification) and read out a few to the class to see if the activities can be guessed.

4 This activity is useful practice for Part 2 of the Speaking paper. Make sure students make notes beforehand (preferably using mindplans) and monitor their discussions, noting areas for improvement.

5/6 Introduce the idea of word stress as shown by the circles, one circle for each syllable, with the large circle showing the main stress. After checking answers, practise pronouncing the words in the completed lists.

If students cope well, you could introduce two other common stress patterns for 2- and 3- syllable words, using words which appear on pages 58 and 59:

oO (e.g. admire, begin, compare, consist, describe, distinct)

oOo (e.g. athletic, creative, determined, guitarist, strategic)

Focus on listening 1 *Student interviews (p.60)*

When students have read the instructions, ask them to work in pairs to predict possible questions and answers, and check ideas briefly. Remind them that thinking about the answers in advance like this helps you listen more effectively. After playing the recording, let students compare answers before checking and, if time allows, focus on interesting expressions, e.g. *swings and roundabouts* (a situation where the disadvantages are balanced by the advantages), *they take your mind off* (your work); (the equipment's) *out of the Ark* (very old or old-fashioned).

Focus on speaking *Leisure activities (p.61)*

1 Read through the *Exam Briefing* as a class and make sure students are clear about the two main elements in a Part 2 topic – **describe** and **explain.** Emphasise that you need to do both well in order to get good marks.

2 Discuss students' ideas, and see if they can think of any additional headings which might be relevant for other activities, e.g. *Costs, Training.*

3 Encourage them to think of appropriate headings for their activity rather than using the ones in the example. Monitor the note-making, helping as necessary.

4 Monitor the conversations while keeping an eye on the time.

5 Monitor discussions and afterwards give feedback and vocabulary input, as appropriate.

Focus on listening 2 *Ten ways to slow down your life (p.62)*

1 Begin by asking students what kind of things cause stress in their lives, and invite a few suggestions for ways of dealing with stress. Then let them read through the *Task Approach.*

2 Clarify the grammatical terms if necessary. A noun phrase is a group of words containing a main noun together with additional information, e.g. *an English language exam/an oral examiner/an exam taken on-line.* Similarly a verb phrase is a group of words associated with a verb, e.g. *take an exam/not turn up for an exam.*
  1 Ask students to study questions 1–4 and underline grammatical clues which help identify the kind of word needed, e.g. *a/the, and.*
  2 To highlight language which is followed by *-ing* forms you could refer students to *Key Language* Exercise 28 on page 230 either before or after the listening task.
After checking answers, you could focus on interesting expressions, e.g. *workload, to skip, clutter, to talk shop, to give* (something) *a miss.*

Focus on writing *Structuring an argument (p.63)*

1/2 Read through the *Task Approach* as a class. Once students have studied the question, have a brief class discussion on the topic to gauge initial reactions. Then let students talk about the points and invite brief feedback.

3/4 Students should work in pairs to discuss these points and draw up mindplans. Ask them to suggest endings for the example sentences in the *Useful language* box and clarify the grammar points as necessary.

5 Remind students that they looked at distinguishing fact from opinion in relation to reading in the previous unit and that this is equally important in their own writing. For question 3, give them time to jot down supporting reasons before inviting a variety of statements.

6 Give students a few minutes to study the paragraph plan, and then check they know what should be included in the three sections. Ask for suggestions for completing the example sentences, e.g. *Nowadays, many families have more than one TV set, and it is common for children to have their own TV set in their bedroom.* Emphasise the academic nature of the task and the importance of register.

7 It would be useful to include the planning phase in class, if time permits, so that you can monitor weaker students' work.

NB There is an exam task on structuring an argument in the *Writing Practice Bank*. This would make suitable follow-up practice to the task here.

8 Remind students to note down the errors they've made in this task, and to make a point of studying the information in the *Error Hit List* on page 66 very carefully. They should also be keeping a record of problem areas.

KEY LANGUAGE

* **Cohesion: reference links**
  Exercise 10, page 217

WRITING PRACTICE

* **Structuring an argument (exam task)**
  Exercise 5, page 239

Unit 6 Key

Focus on vocabulary (p.59)

2 A Volleyball player   **B** Chess player
C Weight trainer   **D** Guitarist   **E** Kayaker

3 Backpacker (*Example answers*)
adventurous, carefree, casual, free, fun, fun loving, likes scenic beauty, loves fresh air, nature lover, needs to get away from society, outdoor type, relaxed, sociable

5 1-syllable words: air, good, health, straight, type
2-syllable words: conscious, outdoor, patient, problem, scenic
3-syllable words: concentrate, logical, physical, sociable, volleyball

Focus on listening 1 (p.60)

1 Computer Studies   **2** on campus   **3** Film Society
4 (a) new gym   **5** cooking   **6** Jim Maybury
7 Athletics Club   **8** a bit limited   **9** (a) swimming pool   **10** playing/plays the guitar

Focus on speaking (p.61)

1 three to four description points (the two *whats* can be combined) and one explanation point

2 (*Example answers*)
1 Time   **2** Benefits   **3** Place   **4** Equipment

Focus on listening 2 (p.62)

2 1 1, 2: noun/noun phrase (following indefinite article); 3: plural noun (following two other plural nouns in a list); 4: noun/noun phrase (following definite article)

2 7: -*ing* form (after preposition and before object); 8: noun/-*ing* form (following definite article)

3 1 finishing time   **2** lunch break   **3** phone calls
4 wastepaper bin   **5** (your/the) in-tray   **6** outside work   **7** listening to   **8** watching television/TV
9 local community   **10** musical instrument

Focus on writing (p.63)

3 (*Example answers*)
1 lack of physical exercise, lack of social contact, lack of mental stimulation
2 computer skills, learning through educational programmes, relaxation
3 taking part in sporting activities (physical exercise), spending time with friends (socialisation), reading (reading skills and vocabulary building)

4 1 *because* is followed by a clause; *because of* is followed by a noun or pronoun   **2** *so* is followed by an adjective (without a noun) or by an adverb; *such* is followed by a noun (with or without an adjective)

5 1 *arguably* (para 1), *suggested* (para 2)
2 (*Example answers*)
The findings of a survey; the large number of workers who take time off for reasons of stress; the small percentage of junior managers who enjoyed their work.
3 (*Example answers*)
* **One reason for this is** that they may spend the money unwisely. **Another (reason) is** that they won't develop a responsible attitude towards money.
* **In the first place**, you can make and receive calls wherever you are. **In addition**, you don't need to have the right change to put in a call box.

8 1 … on t͟h͟e͟ television …   **2** … l͟i͟s͟t͟e͟n͟ to the radio …   **3** … w͟a͟t͟c͟h͟i͟n͟g͟ television …   **4** … playing t͟h͟e͟ piano …   **5** ✓   **6** … listen t͟o͟ the radio …   **7** … concentrate o͟n͟ your driving …   **8** ✓

Reflective Learning 2 (p.67)

Useful vocabulary: priority, adjust, encounter

1 It would be helpful to give an example here, real or invented, of your own aims in studying a particular language, so that students can see the kind of details they need to think about. Give them time to jot down their aims and compare notes, then discuss as a class.

2 Read through the instructions and make sure students are clear about the procedure. This is an **individual** task. Give them plenty of time to complete the task,

making yourself available to discuss and help as necessary. You could look through the completed checklists but it's not really appropriate for students to compare results.

3/4 Monitor the learning goals that students list, advising as necessary. Ask them to report back on their progress towards the three goals they set for *Reflective Learning 1*. Emphasise the positive and focus on any success, however small. Offer advice and encouragement as necessary.

7 ▶ Retail therapy

To set the ball rolling ...

You could explore the idea of shopping as therapy using the following quotation as a springboard: *I always say shopping is cheaper than a psychiatrist.* (Tammy Faye Bakker) Ask if students agree nor not, and why, and develop a discussion around various ways of cheering yourself up when you are feeling down or depressed.

Alternatively, you could look at broader aspects of shopping and consumerism, based on a discussion of one or more of the quotations below.

• *Whoever said money can't buy happiness simply didn't know where to go shopping.* Bo Derek (actress)

• *Too many people spend money they haven't earned, to buy things they don't want, to impress people they don't like.* Will Rogers (comedian)

• *You aren't wealthy until you have something money can't buy.* Garth Brooks (musician)

Lead-in *(p.68)*

1 Let students work through exercise 1 and check their answers, then invite class feedback as to how true they feel the statements are.

Look at any interesting vocabulary, including the following which are from the *Academic Word List: defined, specific, seek, input.*

KEY LANGUAGE

• **Linking expressions**
  Exercise 11, page 219

Focus on speaking 1 *Discussing likes and dislikes; consumer topics (p.68)*

1 Read through the *Exam Briefing* and then focus on the *Useful language* box, in particular the **introductory** and **softening phrases**.

Write a few deliberately general questions on the board, e.g. *Do you like music? Is it important for children to play games? Do people have more freedom these days compared with the past?* Let students realise how difficult they are to answer, then show how the introductory phrase *It depends ...* can be used to help define your terms, e.g. *It depends what kind of music. For example, I love ... but I can't stand ....*

Remind students about the fluency markers they met in Unit 1, e.g. *Well, really, just, actually* and their

importance in making a speaker sound natural. Then explain how they can be used in softening phrases to make negative statements more acceptable. Illustrate with a few negative statements: e.g. *I don't like sport. It's a difficult question. You don't understand.* Show how softening phrases can be used both at beginning and end of sentences and practise as necessary, paying attention to appropriate stress and intonation.

2/3 Arrange students in pairs or groups of three for this practice and monitor their conversations, noting any language which needs attention To round off after each one, ask a few students to report back on their partner's preferences and views.

Focus on reading *Retail therapy (p.69)*

It's worth spending a little time on the issue of long texts and how to tackle them, since it is such a key exam skill. Ask students to suggest how long they think it takes to read a 900-word text, and if you feel the point needs emphasising, and you have time, get them to experiment with a text of roughly that length. The message is that detailed reading of three texts is simply not possible in the 60-minute time limit.

1 For this task, it's very important to set a time limit of just a few minutes. Hopefully, the right choice of answer will encourage students to trust the sampling approach. If students are in any doubt about the correct answer, encourage them to work towards it by eliminating the wrong answers. Emphasise the need to look at the text as a whole, and examine ways that wrong answers contain only partial truth.

2 Again, this task should be completed quickly, without detailed reading, following the guidelines in the *Task Approach*.

3/4 Read through the *Task Approach*, and emphasise the message that parts of speech are a useful tool in this exam task.

Check that students understand the abbreviations. The best approach is probably to work sentence by sentence, identifying the parts of speech needed and selecting from the options. To make the task easier, you could ask students to identify the part of speech of each word in the list of options before they begin.

Do the first question as an example, showing how, once you've identified answers which are grammatically possible (*consumers, scientists*), you only have to choose the most logical one, which you can then check in the relevant part of the text. If you feel your students still need support at this stage, complete the whole exercise as a class.

Afterwards, point out how narrowing the choice for each gap makes the task becomes much easier. Explain that although this introduction may have taken some time, identifying and matching parts of speech should become much quicker and easier as they progress.

5 Ask students to follow the same procedure for this exam task. Explain that the passage includes two extra parts of speech, an adjective (Adj) and adverb (Adv), and check that they are familiar with these. When checking answers, ask students to justify their answers by reference to the text.

6 Refer students back to the *Exam Briefing* on page 32 if necessary. Ask them to follow the advice in the *Reminders*, beginning by highlighting the various journals in the text and underlining key words in questions. Let students compare results before proceeding. When checking answers, ask students to identify the relevant paragraph and parallel expression, so as to eliminate any element of guesswork and underline the need for close, careful reading of the text.

7/8 Read through the *Task Approach* and check understanding of the difference between False and Not Given answers. As a class, analyse the examples given, and make sure students are quite clear about the reason for the Not Given answer in each case. During the checking phase, ask students to justify their answers by reference to the text.

9/10 Talk through the introduction and discuss the meaning of *craving*. Then let students tackle exercise 10, either in pairs or individually. Make sure they locate each expression in the text and look carefully at the context when they do this task.

KEY LANGUAGE
• **Talking about research** Exercise 12, page 219

Focus on vocabulary *Business and Economics (p.74)*

NB All the expressions listed in exercise 1 come from the Topic Activator section of the *Longman Exams Dictionary*.

1/2 To make the task easier, tell students they should look for 4 words in each group. NB Some items could be in more than one group, e.g. *debt* could be in group B or group C depending on whether it is personal or national debt. Check meanings carefully and then ask students to complete exercise 2.

3 Practise the three sounds with more examples if necessary. You could help students by telling them that there should be five words in each group. Let students compare answers and then practise orally after checking.

KEY LANGUAGE
• **Noun + noun combinations** Exercise 13, page 220

Focus on speaking 2 *Describing objects (p.75)*

1 Once the answers have been established, ask students to underline expressions used to describe size, shape and material, and focus on any other useful language, e.g. *They come in pairs.*

2 Draw students' attention to the exam tip and explain it isn't necessary to use 'correct' technical vocabulary, as long as you can find a way of making the meaning clear to the listener. Give students time to study the *Useful language* and point out that expressions like *roughly* and *sort of* can be particularly useful. NB It's worth mentioning that this language is also relevant to description tasks in Task 1 of the Writing paper.

If you want to go into more detail you could include: **colours**: *light/pale* vs *dark/deep*, the use of the suffix *-ish*, e.g. *a brownish shade*; **materials**: *made of* vs *made from*; the suffix *-en*, e.g. *wooden, woollen.*

3 If you have time, you could usefully extend this activity to include objects in other categories, e.g. *clothes, furniture, buildings.*

4 Give students time to read the topic card, and remind them about the two key aspects: **describe** and **explain**. Make sure they all have notes to work from before beginning, and then monitor the pair work. Give feedback to round off.

Unit 7 Key

Lead-in (p.68)
1 See Student's Book, page 253
3 **1** on the other hand,   **2** Meanwhile,   **3** Generally speaking, However,

Focus on reading (p.69)
1 D
2 **1** anticipation (para 2)
   2 brain scan studies (para 3)
   3 New York University (para 4)
4 **1** Npl (subject, of plural verb); Scientists
   2 Ns (follows indefinite article); shopaholic
   3 Npl (subject, of plural verb); consumers
   4 V + -ing (follows preposition); resisting
   5 Ns (part of noun phrase preceding singular verb); condition
   6 V + -ed (past participle, part of passive construction); administered
   7 Number 8.9%
   8 V + -ing (part of present participle); living
   9 V (part of to infinitive); recognise
   10 V (follows modal auxiliary); seek
5 **4** I (Ns – subject/field of study, para 6)
   5 O (Npl – type of professionals, para 3)
   6 A (adj – type of publication where results of research might be published. Could also be Npl, but no matching answer)
   7 K (Npl – contrasts with alone, para 6)
   8 J (Ns – matches financial difficulty para 7. Could also be adj but no matching answer)
   9 G (V+ -ed – past participle, collates with research, para 1)
   10 E (V – followed by object + to + in, para 1)
   11 F (linking word, – matches The good news is, para 1)
   12 P (Ns/Npl, para 1)
6   **13** B (para 4)
     14 A (para 6)
     15 C (para 5)
     16 D (para 7)
     17 A (para 2)
8 **1a** F (the correct figure is <u>about half</u>); **1b** NG (not mentioned in text)
   2a NG (not mentioned in text although it happens to be true); **2b** F (the term comes from the <u>social sciences</u>, not the author)
   18 T para 2: shoppers focused on whether the object … was a bargain
   19 NG
   20 F para 3: Once an item has been purchased, the chemical high dissipates rapidly
   21 F para 4 … real currency is the only thing that gives you the 'pain of paying'. Credit cards might not only anaesthetise pain …
   22 NG

9 In the first example, *a physical craving*, we learn that craving is a sensation which is felt when a person wants to experience the effect (high) of a drug (dopamine). In the second example, *satisfy the craving*, it is used in relation to the feeling of being strongly attracted to food by a delicious smell. Meaning: a feeling of strong desire for something.
10 (*Example answers*)
   1 to think about something in the opposite way to the way originally intended
   2 to become weaker or disappear. (Can also include the idea of wasting something valuable, e.g. money, time or energy)
   3 to force (somebody to do something) (If you are *compelled* to do something, you have no choice but to do it. NB a *compelling* reason or argument is a convincing one that you cannot ignore)
   4 not living (examples of *inanimate objects* include stones, furniture, clothes)
   5 likely (to behave in a particular way)

Focus on vocabulary (p.74)
1 **A** manufacturer, multinational (corporation), retailer, service industry
   B bankruptcy, debt, loss, profit
   C currency, gross national product, inflation, recession
2 **1** manufacturer
   2 retailer
   3 multinationals
   4 service industries
   5 inflation
   6 currency
   7 debt
   8 bankruptcy
3 /ɒ/ gone, loss, odd, profit, wrong
   /əʊ/ flow, gross, home, know, own
   /ʌ/ among, company, done, front, money

Focus on speaking 2 (p.75)
1 **A** eating (with); chopsticks
   B sewing/mending; a needle
   C calculating/adding up, etc.; a calculator

8 ▶ What's on

To set the ball rolling ...

Minimal introduction is needed, but you could ask when students last went to a cinema, theatre or concert, and briefly discuss cultural attractions in the town or city where you are.

Lead-in *(p.78)*

1 To make the task easier, point out that there are five words in each category. Ask students to compare their answers before checking and clarify meanings as necessary.

2 This is a simple awareness-raising exercise. Point out that being aware of word stress patterns is not only relevant to speaking skills, but also an important listening skill.

Some students may still need practice in identifying the number of syllables. If so, begin with the 1-syllable words from the list (five), and then move on to 2-syllable words (five) – no need to differentiate between stress patterns in these. Excluding two-word expressions, this leaves eight three-syllable words for students to work on. When you've checked the answers, practise these orally.

Focus on speaking 1 *Discussing cultural attractions (p.78)*

Focus first on the *Useful language*. Sentences beginning: *The thing ...* or *What ...* are examples of *cleft sentences*. These help the speaker to emphasise a particular part of the sentence – the name comes from the verb *cleave*, which means 'divide into two', because the sentence forms two parts. Cleft sentences are very common in spoken English and they are a good way of showing your ability to use different structures in the Interview.

Illustrate the difference between normal sentence structure and cleft sentences and show how this places extra emphasis on a particular element.

- **What I remember most** about the film was the gunfight.
- **What I liked most** about her was her sense of humour.

It would be useful to have brief oral practice using these structures based on a different occasion, e.g. first day at work/school.

Check that students remember the procedure for Part 2 of the Interview and are equipped to make notes. Divide them into pairs or groups and allow a short time for preparation. Ask them to time each other and stop each speaker after 2 minutes. Monitor the practice and don't let it run on beyond its useful life. Afterwards, ask students to report back briefly and give general feedback.

Optional activity

1 (Pairs/groups) Ask students to explain which two cultural attractions they would recommend a visitor to their country to make a point of visiting, and why.

2 (Pairs) Give students the following list of museums and galleries (all in the London area). Ask them to each choose a museum they would like to visit. They should then explain to their partner the reasons for their choice and try to agree on an attraction to visit together.

pianos	postal history	Sigmund Freud
childhood	ethnology	contemporary art
taxicabs	butterflies	motor cars
astronomy	silk	maritime history

Focus on listening 1 *Music festival (p.79)*

Give students time to read through the introduction and *Task Approach*, and study the questions. To reinforce this advice, check the pronunciation of the items listed in question 1. You could also ask what kind of information is needed for questions 4, 5 and 8. Let students compare answers before checking.

Focus on listening 2 *The Museum of Anthropology (p.80)*

Read through the *Exam Briefing* as a class and check the terms *floor plan* and *cross section*. Then ask students to study the diagram. Check the word *ramp* (a slope connecting two levels) and point out that it doesn't necessarily matter if there are words on a diagram which they don't know. Thinking about them in advance will help them recognise these features when they hear them.

Give students time to study the other questions, making sure they are clear about the two other task types. Encourage them to think about the type of answer needed for each question in the first section, e.g. question 1: a year; question 2: a number; question 3: a place. When checking, read the section of the recording script containing the answers if necessary.

Focus on writing 1 *Describing tables (p.81)*

1/2 It's often useful to vary the way you describe statistics in tables and other diagrams, and this section practises a number of key expressions. Let students study the table and the example sentences before they work through exercises 1–2.

NB There is a note on the expressions *one in ten* and *nine out of ten* in the *Error Hit List* (page 86).

3 Point out that qualifying expressions are equally useful in describing graphs and other diagrams where it's difficult to be precise about a figure. You could check the difference between *less* (used with uncountable nouns, e.g. *less time*) and *fewer* (used with countable nouns, e.g. *fewer people*) either before the exercise or when checking question 5.

4 Students can either work individually or in pairs to complete this task, which is designed to practise 'reading' data from graphs and tables.

5 Give students a few minutes to study the table, and then ask questions to check their interpretation of the data, e.g.:

- *What does the table show?* (attendance at different types of arts events in the UK, by age)
- *How many age groups are included?* (four)
- *How many types of arts events are included?* (six)
- *What is the timescale?* (12 months)
- *What do the figures in the table represent?* (percentages)
- *What type of event was most popular with the youngest age group?* (live music)
- *Was this type of event equally popular with other age groups?* (No, the other age groups preferred theatre performances and carnival and street art to live music events)
- *What were the least popular arts events?* (classical music performances and craft exhibitions)

Give students time to complete the text and compare answers.

NB The following two tasks provide additional relevant practice. They can either be tackled in class or set for homework. The first is an exam writing task based on a table of data, while the second is language practice focusing on the important area of cohesion in writing.

WRITING PRACTICE

- **Describing information from a table (guided practice)**
  Exercise 6, page 240

Remind students to study the *Task Approach* on page 82 before they start. To provide extra support, you might also want to go through the focus questions as a class.
Answers:
1 The number of visits to the UK by overseas residents in the period 1975 to 1998.
2 A steady increase
3 It's almost trebled
4 Leisure
5 Western Europe
6 It's more than doubled.
7 It's more than trebled.
8 No, the leisure sector has decreased slightly.

KEY LANGUAGE

- **Cohesion: avoiding repetition**
  Exercise 14, page 220

Focus on writing 2 *Presenting and justifying an opinion (p.83)*

1/2/3 It would be useful to give students practice with each set of expressions before they progress to exercise 2. Make one or two more assertions to prompt each type of response, e.g. *Childhood is the happiest time of your life. Anyone who breaks the law deserves to go to prison.*

NB If you feel your students need practice in forming conditionals, ask them to do *Key Language* Exercise 15 either before or after exercise 3.

4 See if students can remember the basic approach to Task 2. If not, refer them back to the *Task Approach* for structuring an argument on page 63. Ask students to read through the question and identify the key points. Discuss some possible reasons for disagreement, and some of the implications of the argument. It would be helpful to include the planning phase in class time if possible, so that students can exchange ideas and you can monitor their drafting of paragraph plans.

5 Remind students to note down the errors they've made in this correction task, and to make a point of studying the information in the *Error Hit List* on page 86 very carefully. They should also be keeping a record of problem areas.

KEY LANGUAGE

- **Conditionals**
  Exercise 15, page 221

WRITING PRACTICE

- **Presenting and justifying an opinion (example answer)**
  Exercise 7, page 241

Focus on speaking 2 *Describing an event (p.85)*

1 See if students can identify the photos (the Venice carnival and fireworks over Sydney Harbour bridge) and use these as a springboard for this section. Monitor students' discussions, helping with vocabulary, as necessary, and have a brief round-up at the end.

2 Focus first on the *Useful language*. This is important language for students to learn because it's a simple way to get over the slightly awkward moment of beginning the Long turn, and having a foolproof starting point helps build confidence for this part of the interview.

You could usefully practise this language by firing a number of topics at students and letting them give the first one or two sentences of a response, e.g.:

an important day in your life
an important person in your life
a memorable journey
a place you'd like to visit, etc.

Once students have read through the instructions, you could also refresh their memories about the useful language, including cleft sentences (*The thing …, What …,* etc.) from *Focus on speaking 1*. The pairwork practice can be quite relaxed, and there's no need to set a time limit, but it's important to monitor students' performances and give feedback as necessary before they move on to exercise 3.

3 Make sure everyone has decided on a topic and made some notes. You may want to set strict time limits, especially if the exam is looming, but if you can be more flexible, you may find that the discussion runs for quite a lot longer than the exam would allow. Afterwards, ask students to report briefly on what their partner described. Find out if there were any vocabulary 'gaps', and feed in any useful expressions that you've identified while monitoring.

Unit 8 Key

Lead-in (p.78)

1 a) screen, soundtrack, special effects, stunt, subtitles (cast)

b) act, cast, playwright, scenery, stage

c) backing group, composer, conductor, programme, soloist

d) catalogue, collection, exhibit, portrait, sculpture

2 A collection, composer, conductor, exhibit

B catalogue, scenery, soloist, subtitles

Focus on listening 1 (p.79)

1 C, E (in any order)   **2** A   **3** C   **4** 10.30 a.m.
5 £8   **6** Africa Alive   **7** lunch   **8** £14.50
9 Bus Stop Gallery   **10** student card

Focus on listening 2 (p.80)

1 1949   **2** one (1)   **3** Pacific North-West   **4** shop
5 information desk   **6** (the) Great Hall   **7** five (5)
people   **8** by bus/on a bus   **9** Mondays
10 all year (round)

Focus on writing 1 (p.81)

1 **1** a fifth/20% were 'Very satisfied' and just over half/50% were 'Satisfied'   **2** one per cent/one in 100   **3** five per cent/five in 100

2 **1** a tenth/one in ten   **2** a fifth/one in five **3** a quarter/one in four   **4** a third/one in three **5** three-quarters/three out of four   **6** nine out of ten (only possible answer)

3 **1** just under half/50%   **2** one in three; (exactly) a third   **3** just over half/50%   **4** approximately/ about two thirds   **5** less than ten per cent/fewer than one in ten   **6** almost/approximately/about three quarters/75%

4 **1 a)** (*suggested answers*) 80%
b) (approximately) 65%
c) 40%
d) (approximately) 78%; just under 80%

2 Mobile phone; by 60%

3 Tumble drier; by about 8%

4 20% of British people owned a mobile phone in 1997/98. By comparison, about 30% of the population owned a home computer. By 2006, mobile phone ownership had risen to 80% and home computer ownership to about 68%.

5 **1** 36 %/per cent/just over a third
2 8 %/per cent/less than ten per cent/less than one in ten
3 45–64
4 live musical events (NB plural, followed by the verb *were*)
5 34 %/per cent
6 between
7 four times
8 than

Focus on writing 2 (p.83)

5 **1** … is a good health …   **2** ✓   **3** It is worth pointing out …   **4** an increase in interest …
5 ✓   **6** At the end of the period …   **7** It may be true …   **8** two and a quarter kilometres …
9 ✓   **10** … in the end …

Critical Thinking 2 (p.87)

Useful vocabulary: put forward, sound (adj), thesis, support/supporting, evidence, conclusion, signal/ signalling

Read through the first two sections, giving examples to illustrate the two structures, e.g.

*The President should cancel his visit to China **because of** the financial crisis at home.* (**thesis-led**)

*It is only mild infection **so** it is no cause for concern.* (**evidence-led**)

Check key vocabulary to make sure there's no confusion about the meanings in this context: *argument* = an opinion supported by reasons (not a disagreement); *conclusion* = an opinion reached after considering all the evidence (not the final part of something, e.g. an essay).

1 In extracts 1 and 4, ask students to point out the thesis statement and evidence, and to identify each argument as **thesis-led** or **evidence-led**. In extracts 2 and 3, ask them to suggest a suitable thesis statement. In extract 5, ask them to suggest suitable evidence.

2 This is best done as pair work, with students reporting back afterwards. It would be useful for them to write a few examples of both **thesis-led** and **evidence-led** arguments as a record.

Key: See Student's Book, page 259.

9 ▶ Water, water everywhere

To set the ball rolling ...

Ask students to suggest a few of the world's valuable resources, e.g. gold, silver, oil and, hopefully, water. Then ask which is the most precious and why. Establish that life on Earth depends on water, and perhaps extend with a few trivia questions, e.g. *What percentage of water do our bodies contain?* (60–70%); *How long can human beings survive without water?* (no more than five to six days or two to three days in a hot climate).

Lead-in *(p.88)*

1 Use the first pair of activities as an example if necessary. You could also ask students to guess how many litres each activity uses. Then give them a couple of minutes to discuss the other pairs. As they check the answers, ask students to write the number of litres used next to each activity.

2 Read through the instructions and ask students to study the bar chart.

Ask a few questions to check that they can read it, e.g. *Which food is mentioned? How much water does it take to produce one serving of tomatoes? How many other foods are included in the chart?*

If necessary, help weaker students get started by directing them to the third or fourth sentences, which provide a comparison with tomatoes. After checking the answers, focus on key language. Ask students to underline the comparatives used in the four sentences, and then highlight these structures on the board, together with qualifiers. NB This language is also set out in *Key Language* Exercise 7, page 214.

twice/three times **as much/many ... as**
50% **more ... than**
half/a quarter of/a third of ...

nearly/(slightly) less than/(just) under
(slightly) more than/(just) over
about/approximately

For further practice, you could ask students to compare: *tomatoes/oranges*; *oranges/pasta*; *pasta/chicken*.

3 There is plenty of scope for error with these comparatives, especially if students try to mix and match components, e.g. *a half more*. To avoid confusion and complicated explanations, encourage students to stick strictly to the three structures from the previous exercise.

Begin by eliciting endings for two example patterns, e.g.

*Taking a shower uses nearly **twice as much water as** using a dishwasher.*

*It takes over **50% more water** to take a shower **than** to use a dishwasher.*

Focus on the use of the verbs *take* and *use* (*It takes .../X uses*), pointing out that they are not interchangeable, and also on the use of the *-ing* form and infinitive.

Add an additional example to remind students about the use of fractions, e.g.

*Taking a shower uses **three-quarters of the water** (which is) needed to take a bath.*

Focus on speaking *Water issues (p.89)*

1 Depending on time, either answer these quickly as a class or in more depth as pairwork, followed by class discussion.

2 NB You could usefully focus on **language of speculation** before students begin the quiz:

*(I think) the answer **could/might/may be** ... because ...*

For example ask: *Which country in the world has the highest ratio of cars to people?* (USA, with 570 cars to every 1,000 persons); *Where is the world's driest place?* (The Atacama Desert, Chile).

Tell students that even though they may not know the answers, they should discuss the options and choose the most likely answers.

Monitor students' conversations to make sure they are speculating and giving reasons. Afterwards, invite ideas on a few questions, without accepting or rejecting answers, since these can be found in the following text.

Focus on reading 1 *Water: Earth's most precious resource (p.90)*

NB Although a typical exam reading passage would not include information in tables in this way, the task is designed to practise skimming and scanning skills.

Read through the notes and then set students a time limit (say 4 to 5 minutes) to find the necessary information. When checking answers, ask students to identify the relevant section of text.

If time allows, you may want to exploit the figures for language practice and/or pick up on useful language, e.g. *to increase* **sevenfold**, **by 35 times**, **by more than half**; **plentiful**; **from** *a health* **point of view**; **accounting for** *as much as 80%.*

Focus on reading 2 *The Ecology of Hollywood (p.91)*

1/2 This is a long text so it's particularly important to reinforce the skills of skimming and scanning and to read in detail only when necessary. Remind students about the technique of sampling a text, which was introduced in Unit 7 (page 70), and give them a few minutes to do this. Then let them read through the *Task Approach* and study the table.

Give them time to scan the text and find and highlight the first topic (Los Angeles Aqueduct) before studying the information. You may need to help weaker students to locate the references to other aqueducts. As it's quite a challenging task, it's advisable to monitor students' work closely and give a helping hand, as necessary. Let students compare answers before checking thoroughly, by reference to the text.

3 Matching tasks were introduced in Unit 3 (page 32). Read through the *Reminders* and ask students to study the question and underline key words or phrases in each problem. Check vocabulary if necessary, e.g. *adverse, inadequate.* They should have already highlighted the aqueducts, but will need to find and highlight the reference to *extraction* as well (para 6).

Monitor students' work, helping as necessary, and ask them to underline the phrases in the text which match the problems. Again, let them compare answers before checking thoroughly by reference to the text.

4 Sentence-completion tasks were introduced in Unit 3 (page 33). Read through the *Reminders*, and check that students follow the recommended procedure. Check answers thoroughly, by reference to the text.

5 Multiple-choice tasks were introduced in Unit 5 (page 52), and it's worth checking that students remember the *Task Approach,* in particular, the three key questions: *Is it mentioned in the text? Is it true? Is it relevant?* You could help weaker students by telling them they need to focus on paras 8–10 of the text.

When checking answers, ask students to say why the wrong answers are wrong, i.e.

A Not true – waste water is being recycled. (para 10)

D Not true – this was suggested (para 8) but now the plan is to restore the river. (para 9)

E Not true – the agencies already exist. (para 9)

G Not mentioned in the text.

NB There are a number of relative pronouns in the reading text and there is a *Key language* exercise focusing on this important area of language which could usefully be done in class, if time allows, or for homework.

KEY LANGUAGE

- **Relative clauses**
  e.g. The LA river, which stretches 92 kilometres …
  Exercise 16, page 222

Focus on vocabulary *(p.95)*

NB The text contains a number of common expressions for introducing sentences such as *Surprisingly, Paradoxically* and *Inevitably.* These and other expressions are practised in *Key Language* Exercise 17 (see below).

1 The aim is to encourage students to make intelligent guesses about the meaning of difficult or unusual words and expressions. Make sure students do look for the expressions in the text and study the context, rather than simply guess. When checking, clarify meaning and use with extra examples, as necessary.

2 In some cases, it's easy to say which noun or verb the adjective is derived from, e.g. *ecology/ecological,* but in others, the derivation is less transparent. This exercise is best done in class, since students can then be encouraged to add to the list and/or suggest other topic areas, particularly from their own specialisation.

NB There is *Key Language* practice in this area of language.

KEY LANGUAGE

- **Introducing sentences**
  Exercise 17, page 223
- **Word building: nouns**
  Exercise 18, page 223

Unit 9 Key

Lead-in *(p.88)*
1 See Student's Book, page 254.
2 The missing foods, from left to right: oranges, pasta, milk, chicken.
3 (*Example answers*)
  1 Taking a bath uses more than 30% more water than taking a shower.
  2 It takes seven times more water to use a dishwasher than to wash dishes by hand.
  3 We use ten times as much water for cooking each day as for drinking.
  4 It takes over three times as much water to water the garden as to wash the car. / Washing the car uses less than a third of the water needed to water the garden.

Focus on reading 1 *(p.90)*
2 1 a) (Figure 2)
  2 80 (Text after Figure 3)
  3 USA, Japan (highest); India (lowest) (Figure 3)
  4 70% (Text after Figure 1)
  5 e.g. glaciers, aquifers, lakes, etc. (Figure 1)
  NB It's worth introducing the term *aquifer*, since it occurs again in the main text: an *aquifer* is any rock formation containing water that can be used to supply wells.
  6 a) (Text after Figure 1)
  7 c) (Text after Figure 4)
  8 c) (most); b) (least) (Figure 4)

Focus on reading 2 *(p.91)*
2 1 1941 (para 5) **2** 350km (4) **3** Mono Lake (5)
3 4 B *Within ten years, the city needed more.* (para 5)
  5 D *LA's entitlement was reduced by about 50%* (5)
  6 A *with inevitably harmful consequences for fish and wildlife* (5)
  7 C *40 per cent of the wells … contaminated above federal limits* (6)
4 8 J *respiratory problems due to vehicle emissions* (para 2)
  9 A *No metropolis on the planet has looked further afield for its supply* (4)
  10 G *the considerable winter rainfall … is swallowed by concrete drainage systems …* (6)
  11 B *a threat to economic expansion* (7)
5 (Answers can be in any order)
  B *nature walks … equestrian trails* (9)
  C *to collect run-off rainwater from buildings, and redirect it …* (10)
  F *to restore the river* (9)

Focus on vocabulary *(p.95)*
1 1 d **2** e **3** a **4** c **5** b
2 1 F **2** H **3** G **4** A **5** C **6** D **7** E **8** B
3 1 underway
  2 urban
  3 ecological
  4 federal
  5 disparate
  6 inevitably
  7 support
  8 economic

10 ▶ Hazard warning

To set the ball rolling ...

Use part 1 of the *Lead-in* as the springboard to a discussion about risk and attitudes to risk.

Note on photograph: In 1974, Philippe Petit, a French high wire artist, walked across a tightrope between the World Trade Center's Twin Towers, New York. The stunt was called "The Artistic Crime of the Century" by *Time* magazine. Petit used a 7.9 m long balancing pole and walked the wire for 45 minutes, making eight crossings between the towers before giving himself up to the police. He was arrested but charges against him were later dropped. A documentary film called *Man on Wire* about this event has won many awards.

Lead-in *(p.98)*

1 Once students have answered questions 1–3, develop the discussion further. Ask how they would describe Philippe Petit's action and if they think he should have been prosecuted (see notes above). Ask what other dangerous sports students can think of. Examples include obvious ones like rock climbing, cave diving and motorcycling, but also some less obvious ones which carry unexpected risk such as horse riding (128 deaths per 100,000 compared with only 1.3 per 100,000 for boxing!) and cycling (more children break bones riding bicycles than in any other sport). What is the appeal of such activities? Should dangerous sports be banned? Why/Why not?

2 Arrange students in pairs and explain that they have 10 minutes for the task so there is plenty of time for discussion. They should take it in turns to answer each question, giving reasons or explaining circumstances in each case. Partners should listen carefully and ask questions. Monitor their conversations, helping with vocabulary if necessary, e.g. *resign, white water rafting* and noting any language areas that need attention. Once students have checked their scores, ask how accurate they think they are and invite them to report back on the most interesting things they've learnt about their partner.

3 Let students stay in pairs to discuss these exam-style topics. Again, monitor and provide feedback on language issues as appropriate.

Focus on speaking 1 *Natural hazards (p.99)*

It's useful to begin by focusing on the term *natural hazard*. Ask students to look at the examples in the box and establish that these are extreme natural events, which are likely to cause serious loss of life and destruction of property when they occur in a populated area. You could ask students to suggest three main causes (climatic, geological, land instability). Point out that the topic, which crosses several disciplines including geography and geology, is an increasingly popular field of study.

NB It has been estimated that natural hazards are responsible for 250,000 deaths and US$40 billion of damage each year.

1 Clarify any vocabulary students are unsure about. NB *tropical cyclones* are the same as *hurricanes* and *typhoons* (violent revolving storms with high winds, usually occurring in the tropics). *Tornados* are swirling columns of wind, common in the central USA. Allow a few minutes for the discussion, and then invite brief feedback.

Optional topic vocabulary practice
Ask students to put the following words under the correct heading: A Volcano or B Earthquake. Use the checking phase to clarify meanings, as necessary. *active, aftershock, crater, dormant, epicentre, erupt, extinct, fault line, seismic, tremor*
Key: **A:** active, crater, dormant, erupt, extinct; **B:** aftershock, epicentre, fault line, seismic, tremor

---

2 Practise the two sounds with more examples if necessary. Let students compare answers and then practise orally after checking.

3 NB It may be helpful for students to practise expressions of cause and result before beginning this task (see *Key Language*, Exercise 19, page 224).

Make sure students understand the concept of grading natural hazards in terms of the severity of their impact, and discuss each of the factors briefly beforehand. Invite feedback after the pairwork, and develop the discussion to include relevant issues and vocabulary, such as warning time, population density (*densely/ sparsely populated*), and effects on infrastructure (*communication failures; closure of schools and airports*, etc.). Finally, let students refer to the official ranking on page 254. If you have time, you could use the table for practice in interpreting statistical information, e.g. *Which events – cause the greatest loss of life? – affect the largest area? – have the greatest social effect?*

KEY LANGUAGE

- **Expressing cause and result**
  Exercise 19, page 224
This exercise practises a number of expressions which are useful in talking and writing about this topic. Given the possible pitfalls where grammar is concerned, the exercise is probably best done in class, except with very able students.

Focus on listening 1 *Predicting a volcanic eruption (p.100)*

Before playing the recording, allow time for studying and discussing the drawings, either in pairs or as a class, and invite a few guesses as to possible answers.

If you have time when checking answers, you could focus on a few interesting expressions, e.g. *I'll have to take your word for it; if I remember rightly.*

NB The recording script provides an opportunity to focus on *the … the …* comparatives (*The bigger it is, the more likelihood there is of an eruption*), which are practised in *Key Language* Exercise 23, page 227. However, this language point is referenced in Unit 12, and you may prefer to wait until then.

Focus on listening 2 *Tsunami (p.101)*

Remind students about the importance of scanning instructions and questions in advance when there are several task-types like these, and you need to adapt quickly.

Make sure they notice how the numbers run (clockwise). Check pronunciation of the words in the list A–F, and remind students of the advice from Unit 8: to say words silently in advance so they are easier to recognise on the recording.

If you have time when checking answers, you could focus on one or two useful expressions, e.g. *mean* (= average), *one-storey* (+ *single-storey, two-storey, multi-storey*).

Focus on writing *Describing a process (p.102)*

1/2 Give students time to read through the *Exam Briefing* and then ask them to repeat the three criteria for assessment.

When students have read the *Task Approach* and studied the diagram, ask them to suggest a suitable starting point for the description (there's no particular need for consensus on this), and then to attempt to describe the process simply in their own words. It may be helpful to revise the use of passives (*Key Language* Exercise 5, page 212) (but note the danger of overusing passives – see notes on question 5 below).

Discuss and agree a suitable introduction and make sure students write this at the beginning of the text on page 103.

3/4 With weaker students it may help to go through the first two questions as a class to illustrate the kind of choices of verb form they need to make, i.e. singular/plural? active/passive?

5 It's important that students are clear about when a passive construction is appropriate, and when not, as overuse of the passive is just as much of a problem in academic writing as underuse. Ask them to count examples of the passive in the completed text (3) and compare with examples of the active voice (10). Look at each verb form in turn and discuss why an active or passive is appropriate.

6/7 The aim is to raise awareness of sequence markers and to encourage appropriate use of a good range of these. They should be given a high profile throughout the rest of the unit, both in the writing and speaking sections. NB *At first/first, at last/lastly* and *after/afterwards* feature in the *Error Hit List* on page 106.

8 Allow time for students to study the diagram and ask questions if they wish.

Remind them to try and put notes on the diagram into their own words where possible. They should remember to link sentences appropriately (see page 24) and to mark stages with suitable sequence expressions (see page 103). With weaker students, it may be helpful to run through the description orally first.

NB There is a model answer with focus questions for this task in the *Writing Practice Bank*, see page 42.

9 Although the diagram may look a bit complicated, the process should be fairly easy to follow and the necessary topic vocabulary is supplied. Clarify this as necessary:

dough is a mixture of flour and water used to make bread. The word is used here to describe a mixture with a similar texture or 'feel'. Clarify the pronunciation /dəʊ/, pointing out that *dough* rhymes with *so* or *although*.

lead is a soft heavy grey metal used to cover roofs or in pencils for writing. Clarify the pronunciation /led/, pointing out that *lead* (the metal) rhymes with *bed* or *head*, unlike the verb *lead* /liːd/, which rhymes with *need*.

It would help to talk through the sequence beforehand, making sure students are aware that there are two separate processes (making the pencil leads and making the pencil cases). These come together at the point where the leads are inserted into the wooden slats.

Discuss whether there needs to be more than one paragraph (one is acceptable, but two may be clearer), and remind them of the importance of good linking with appropriate sequence expressions.

With weaker students, you may need to practise describing the process orally first. If students still need help, use the example answer in the Key to give prompts or to prepare a gapped model.

NB There is a gapped model answer for this task in the *Writing Practice Bank*, page 243 (see below), which would be useful remedial practice after students have attempted their own answer. There is also an exam task, exercise 10, which is suitable for extra practice. Alternatively, this could be reserved for revision at a later stage.

WRITING PRACTICE

- **Describing a process (example answer)**
  Exercise 8, page 242
- **Describing a process (guided practice)**
  Exercise 9, page 243
- **Describing a process (exam task)**
  Exercise 10, page 244

Focus on speaking 2 *Describing stages, discussing risk (p.105)*

1 Remind students to note down the errors they've made in correction, and to make a point of studying the information in the *Error Hit List* very carefully. They should also be keeping a record of problem areas so that these can be revised regularly and, hopefully, eliminated! This task will check students' revision as it recycles some errors from earlier *Error Hit Lists*.

2 These topics provide an opportunity to use sequence expressions in speaking. You could remind students of the list on page 103, but point out that the following are quite formal and therefore normally restricted to written English: *subsequently*, *at this stage* and *during this process*. It's a good idea to give an example of what is required first, taking a different topic, e.g. *How I became an English language teacher*.

3 This activity usually generates a lot of discussion and some surprising results!

Make sure students understand the instructions and task before they begin. If you can prepare an OHP transparency or a PowerPoint slide showing the official table on page 254, the answers can be revealed bit by bit, for dramatic effect. Afterwards discuss people's tendency to underestimate voluntary everyday risks, and overestimate more dramatic involuntary risks like floods. What reasons could there be for this?

NB This topic can also be exploited for writing.

WRITING PRACTICE

- **Presenting and justifying an opinion (exam task)**
  Exercise 11, page 245

Unit 10 Key

Lead-in (p.98)

See Student's Book, page 254.
Point out that there are positive aspects to risk taking, which include learning new skills and developing positive thinking. High achievers tend to take more risks in life than other people.

Focus on speaking 1 (p.99)

2 a) brown, doubt, now, round, vowel
b) blood, done, front, rough, won
3 See Student's Book, page 254.

Focus on listening 1 (p.100)

1 height (of cloud)
2 volume (of cloud)
3 drying vegetation
4 landslide
5 mudflow
6 earthquake
7 wells drying (up)
8 abnormal animal behaviour
9 rumbling (sound)
10 sulphur smell

Focus on listening 2 (p.101)

1 C
2 E
3 D
4 earthquake(s)
5 80–90%
6 half a/0.5 metre
7 Russia
8 480km
9 700
10 B

Focus on writing (p.102)

2 B
3 1 causes (the) 2 is released 3 rises 4 are blown
5 reach 6 fall 7 is absorbed 8 runs
4 Present simple and present perfect simple tenses; because we are referring to events which happen repeatedly, all the time.
5 False
6 As, then, until, At this stage, After, eventually
7 1 Meanwhile, During this process, At this stage,
2 Eventually,
3 *First, Finally,* because they indicate the beginning and end of a process, which is inappropriate for a cycle, as it is continuous.
8 See example answer in *Writing Practice*, Exercise 8, page 242.
9 See Guided practice in *Writing Practice*, Exercise 9, page 243.

Focus on speaking 2 (p.105)

1 1 ✓
2 Firstly/First/First of all …
3 … economical …
4 …hours later/afterwards …
5 ✓
6 At first …
7 … an increase in …
8 a large/considerable/substantial amount …
9 … on the television …
10 ✓
3b See Student's Book page 254.

Reflective Learning 3 *(p.107)*

Useful vocabulary: relevant, strategy.

1 Point out that according to research, we find it hard to recall a new vocabulary item after just 12 seconds and it disappears completely after about 20 seconds if it is not repeated or written down. Apparently writing something down tells the brain that this is more important then other bits of information and should be stored in the long-term memory.

Let students work through the questions in pairs and then discuss the different approaches as a class. Topics to touch on include:

- the value of taking personal responsibility for learning; vocabulary you choose yourself is likely to be more relevant to your needs and more memorable than vocabulary from the teacher.
- the importance of being selective when learning vocabulary (they will find out how to identify high frequency words in section 2).
- the need to be systematic in vocabulary learning (see *Language Facts* box.)

Optional activity

To put the three different dictionaries listed in question 2 to a practical test, ask students to choose three new words from Unit 10 and then consult all three (or even just two) before comparing results. Hopefully this will demonstrate the wealth of information available in an English–English dictionary compared with the other two. The plus side where students are concerned is obviously convenience but it's important they are aware of their limitations. Depending on resources, this activity could be done in pairs or as a class.

---

2 Check if students are aware of the IPA (International Phonetic Alphabet). Point out its value as a resource and explain that it is listed in most dictionaries. Clarify the way stress is marked (main stressed syllable preceded by ') and check the other abbreviations.

3 A You could suggest more topics, e.g. *crime, transport, healthcare, work*, etc. and give students 5 minutes to produce their own diagrams, based on the model, and present them to the class.

B Make sure students can identify the different aspects of word knowledge which are illustrated on the reverse of the word card; NB the translation is in Greek. Mention word families and word grammar as additional useful information.

Talk through the **ideas for vocabulary learning**, encouraging students to make suggestions for implementing each one.

4 Remind students of the importance of experimenting with new study strategies. Monitor the learning goals that students list, advising as necessary.

5 Ask them to report back on their progress towards the learning goals they set for *Reflective Learning 2*. Emphasise the positive and focus on any success, however small. Offer advice and encouragement as necessary.

Key: See Student's Book, page 258.

11 ▶ Use it or lose it

To set the ball rolling ...

Ask students to think of something they have to remember that day, e.g. a phone call to make, a bill to pay, where they parked the car! Elicit a few examples and briefly discuss strategies for remembering these things. You could also elicit some topic vocabulary, e.g. *be forgetful, absent-minded, learn by heart, have a photographic memory, jog someone's memory.*

NB This unit (whether covered in one session or more) works particularly well if it is framed by the two parts of the Memory Test. Leaving the last 5 to 10 minutes for Part 2 requires careful timing, but is worthwhile.

Lead-in *(p.108)*

1/2 Start with books closed. Explain how the Memory Test will work, and check that everyone is clear about what they have to do. Tell them they can write words down on a piece of paper if they think this will help. For fairness, ensure that students start and stop studying the words simultaneously. Time the 2 minutes as exactly as possible.

It may be worth checking students lists quickly afterwards to make sure there are no wrong words or wildly wrong spellings. Ask them to make a note of their score for future reference before talking through the discussion points as a class.

3 Encourage students to think of other methods apart from making a written note. Invite feedback after pairwork, and perhaps list a range of strategies on the board.

NB If you have worked through *Reflective Learning 3* (page 107) recently, the last item (new English vocabulary) should be revision. If not, it's worth spending a bit of time on this as a way of highlighting effective strategies for remembering new vocabulary, e.g. recording expressions in a context, a phrase or sentence, rather than in isolation; making a point of revising and using new expressions; grouping words in word families, etc.

If time allows, you could extend the discussion of some of the points and introduce extra topic vocabulary.

Focus on reading 1 *Sleep (p.109)*

1 It may be easiest to discuss the headline if it's written on the board. Otherwise, ask students to cover the article. Check *eve* and *sleep* (noun or verb?) and invite speculation about the general meaning. Afterwards, explain the phrase *to burn the midnight oil*, i.e. to work or study until late at night.

2 Set a time limit for reading of about 1 minute, to discourage detailed reading.

3 Set a time limit of about 2 minutes to reinforce the key element of scanning.

4 You may need to do the first question together, so as to underline the need for an exact match of cause and effect, and also for consistency of tenses. When checking, ask students to justify answers by reference to the text. Question 3 in particular will repay analysis, since it relies on understanding several reference links (see Key).

NB If you have time, you could also look at some vocabulary use in the text, e.g.:

- **metaphorical expressions**, e.g. *to* **cram** *for an exam* (para 1): **cram** means to force something into a small space (e.g. *to cram things into a suitcase*) so the meaning is to study hard and quickly; *to* **nail** *something* **down** (last para): a **nail** is a piece of metal used to fasten things together, so the meaning is to fix it permanently.
- **dependent prepositions**, e.g. *to deprive people* **of** *sleep, to substitute study* **for** *sleep* (included in *Academic Vocabulary 6* (page 117).

Focus on reading 2 *Use it or lose it (p.110)*

1 You may want students to work through all the questions without interruption, especially if the exam is close. If you feel the class needs more support, however, follow the suggested approach below.

2 Let students read through the *Exam Briefing*, and then give them a limited time (say 4 minutes) to answer the questions. Ask them to compare answers before checking.

Optional activity

To allow students to explore the topic further before continuing with the exam questions, write the three categories *Mental Speed* (MS), *Learning Capacity* (LC) and *Working Memory* (WM) on the board. Let students find and study the information about these in the text, and then ask them to discuss which would be involved in the following:

1 using a sophisticated new camera (LC)
2 doing the shopping in a big supermarket (WM)
3 deciding what to do when a frying pan catches fire (MS)
4 finding out how to use the internet (LC)
5 playing a doubles game at tennis (MS)
6 making arrangements for a children's party (WM)

3 Check that students remember how to tackle this task. (If not, refer them to the *Exam Briefing* and *Task Approach* on page 33.) Make sure they underline key words or phrases as they look through the questions (check these if necessary), and ask them to note down the number of the relevant paragraph next to their chosen answer. Check answers together with paragraph references.

4 Let students read through the *Reminders* and highlight the people A–C in the text. Don't point out that A appears twice – deal with this at the checking stage if necessary. Remind students that statements 6–10 are likely to paraphrase information from the text. When checking, ask students to quote relevant paragraph numbers.

For the True/False/Not Given section, remind students, if necessary, that questions are in the same order as the information in the text. When checking, make sure students can justify their answers by reference to the text.

Focus on vocabulary *Word families (p.113)*

1/2 Remind students about the advice on learning and recording vocabulary in *Reflective Learning 3* (page 107), specifically the importance of recording a new word carefully with all relevant information.

These exercises focus on two aspects of this information, word families (a way of learning three words for the price of one, in effect!) and dependent prepositions.

NB The text also provides an opportunity to focus on semi-fixed phrases (i.e. phrases where it's possible to make small variations by adding adjectives and adverbs), and if you have time, you could also look at some of these, e.g.
(partly) **explains why/how** … (para 2)
provides *(even stronger)* **evidence of** … (8)
lead to/point to the *(interesting/intriguing/worrying)* **possibility of that** … (10)
has *(clearly)* **shown** *that* … (10)

KEY LANGUAGE

• **The verb suffix -*en***
Exercise 20, page 225

Focus on speaking *Memories (p.114)*

1 Explain that this is a useful diagnostic exercise, i.e. an opportunity to discover any gaps in their knowledge of articles. Point out that there is one mistake in each sentence. Ask students to compare answers and then give them time to consult *Key Language* Exercise 21 and correct as many errors as possible. After a final check, encourage them to highlight the mistakes they missed or (corrected wrongly) in this exercise, together with the correct versions, for future reference.

KEY LANGUAGE

• **Articles**
Exercise 21, page 225

2 Read through the introduction and, if necessary, review the recommended *Useful language* as a class. Arrange students in pairs and check that they remember the procedure for Part 2 of the Interview.

Allow about a minute for the first 'candidate' to choose a topic and make notes, and then 2 minutes for the Long turn itself. Include as many topics and changes of candidate as time allows. Give general feedback afterwards.

3 Focus on the *Useful language* first and make sure students are clear about the key language patterns, e.g. *Years ago/In the past/When I was a child* / + **past tense**; *Since then* / *Over the last few years* + **present perfect**; *Nowadays* + **present**.

Students should continue the interview format (although you may want to change pairs around). Again, set up time checks and monitor students' work.

4 As with Part 1 of the Memory Test, it's best to run through the instructions with books closed. You can then ensure that everyone has exactly 2 minutes to study the diagrams. Ask students to total their scores for the two parts and see if anyone had significantly better results in one or other part. If time allows, you could check some related language, e.g. *shaped like a rectangle, roughly rectangular in shape*. (See page 75.)

5 Monitor pairwork and have a general round-up discussion, touching on topics like verbal versus visual awareness (question 1), and effective exam preparation (questions 2 and 3).

Unit 11 Key

Focus on reading 1 (p.109)

3 1 the link between sleep and memory
  2 Harvard Medical School
  3 in *Nature Neuroscience* (a scientific journal)
  4 24
  5 a visual discrimination task (involving diagonal lines on a computer screen)

4 1 E (first and second paras)
  2 F (whole article)
  3 D *Those* (volunteers) who *had not* (slept normally), showed *none* (no improvement)
  4 B To eliminate the effects of fatigue … then slept normally …
  5 A Among the group who had slept normally, … a marked improvement.
  6 C (last para)

Focus on reading 2 (p.110)

2 1 B, C, E (in any order)
3 2 C (para 2) **3** F (3) **4** A (5) **5** H (5)
4 1 6 A (7) **7** C (10) **8** A (2) **9** B (8) **10** C (10)
5 11 TRUE (4/5) Absent-mindedness occurs at all ages; Stress … can also cause such absent-mindedness
  12 FALSE (10) mental not physical training
  13 NG
  14 FALSE (11) Why this should be true for memory … is not yet clear

Focus on vocabulary (p.113)

1 1 suspicion
  2 suspicious
  3 decision
  4 decisive
  5 comparison
  6 comparative/comparable
  7 lengthen
  8 length
  9 age
  10 ageing (aging US)/aged
  11 memorise (-ize US)
  12 memorable

2 1 comparison
  2 decisive
  3 memorise
  4 aged
  5 memorable
  6 ageing
  7 lengthen
  8 suspect
3 1 of
  2 to
  3 from
  4 in
  5 to
  6 in
  7 of
  8 to

Focus on speaking (p.114)

1 1 in the United States
  2 for the life
  3 failed the entry test
  4 when I was a child
  5 related to the drugs
  6 the best holiday I ever had
  7 a good health
  8 the first Monday

12 ▶ You live and learn

To set the ball rolling ...

You could discuss one or more of the following quotations:

- *... it is well to remember from time to time that nothing that is worth knowing can be taught.* (Oscar Wilde, Irish playwright and poet)
- *Education is what most people receive, many pass on and few have.* (Karl Kraus, Austrian critic)
- *Education is what survives when what has been learnt has been forgotten.* (B.F. Skinner, American psychologist)

Lead-in *(p.118)*

Education is one of the most predictable topics in the Speaking Test, so it's important that students are clear about relevant vocabulary, particularly expressions relating to their own studies, whether in the past or planned for the future. Be prepared to add vocabulary that is specific to your students' needs.

1/2 Let students work on these two tasks and compare results. Clarify any meanings, as necessary.

- *Fresher* = a student in their first year of study (British English). The US equivalent is *freshman*.
- *Thesis* = a long piece of writing, based on original work, usually prepared for a university postgraduate degree. NB This word occurs in *Focus on writing 2* with a second and less common meaning: an opinion supported by a reasoned argument.

3 Word stress was introduced in Unit 6. If students still need practice in identifying syllables, use the examples as a starting point. Then, from the list in exercise 1, ask them to identify two one-syllable words and a few two- and three-syllable words. Once they're reasonably confident, move on to stress, going back to the examples for practice. When you've checked the answers, practise these orally as well.

Read through the *Language fact* box in class to make sure the pattern is clear. You could also give oral practice using the following words:

- *technology, sociology, meteorology, criminology*
- *variety, complexity, electricity, probability*
- *geography, demography, radiography, oceanography, philosophy*
- *librarian, humanitarian, parliamentarian*
- *geometry, symmetry*
- *educate, calculate, exaggerate, discriminate*
- *astronomy, economy, agronomy*

Focus on speaking 1 *Schooldays (p.119)*

1 Point out the difference between giving answers which are adequate in Part 1 of the test and answers which are excellent. Emphasise the importance of really listening to the question (not giving a prepared answer to a similar question), and using the opportunity to demonstrate a good range of structures and vocabulary.

2 Practise forming questions from the prompts beforehand if necessary. You could also ask one or two preliminary questions to practise the *Useful language*, e.g. *Which was your least favourite subject at school? Why?* or *Who was your best friend at school? What was special about them?*

3 Give students time to study the topics and make notes. Remind them, if necessary, to use key words or phrases (possibly set out in a mindplan) rather than sentences. Monitor, making sure monologues don't slip into dialogues. Afterwards ask a few students to explain briefly what their partners said, and give any relevant language feedback.

Focus on listening 1 *The golden rules of listening (p.120)*

1 Use the questionnaire as a springboard for a brief discussion about listening skills: what helps, what hinders, how to improve, etc. Then let students look through the tasks, and perhaps discuss a few possible answers as a way of encouraging prediction as a routine strategy.

Note on the cartoon: This is a famous saying of Diogenes, a Greek philosopher who became legendary for his rejection of life's comforts – he was reputed to have lived for a time in a barrel.

2 Make sure students look carefully through the questions in advance and encourage them to discuss possible answers for questions 3–10. The recording script contains a number of common collocations, including simple phrases such as *pay attention* and *make a good impression*. If you have time, you could include *Key Language* Exercise 22, which practises similar collocations. Encourage students to keep a careful record of these as they meet them.

KEY LANGUAGE

- **Vocabulary: collocations**
  Exercise 22, page 227

Focus on listening 2 *Making the most of your memory (p.121)*

1/2 Take time to discuss pre-listening questions 1–5 as a class (without providing definitive answers) and point out how important it is to be alert for clues like these.

3 These questions encourage students to reflect on the task and on strategies they used. You could also ask if there was any information in the lecture which they feel they could make use of in their own learning. NB The recording script contains an example of a *the ... the* comparative. There is optional practice in this area of language in *Key Language* Exercise 23.

KEY LANGUAGE

- *The ... the* (comparatives)
  Exercise 23, page 227

Focus on writing 1 *Presenting an opinion (p.122)*

1 This task introduces the **thesis-led** approach as an alternative to the **evidence-led** approach which was discussed in Unit 6. It also looks at linking ideas using expressions of concession or contrast.

2 Briefly discuss students' initial reactions to the exam topic. Give them time to highlight key words or phrases in the question and make notes. If more help is needed, you could talk through some of the issues as a class first, e.g. *What is the purpose of testing (for students and teachers)? What kind of things could teachers do instead if they didn't have to concentrate on exam preparation?*

3/4/5 Begin by revising the basic structure of an **evidence-led** approach. It may be helpful to clarify the meaning of *thesis* here (i.e. an opinion put forward and supported by a reasoned argument), as distinct from its more common meaning discussed earlier in the *Lead-in*. Make sure students are clear about how the two approaches differ, and which situations they are best suited to. Monitor the paragraph planning and let students compare results afterwards.

6/7/8/9 Read through the examples and discuss the questions as a class. For exercise 7, point out that sentences can be combined or not, depending on which linking expression is chosen. It may be helpful to do the first together to illustrate the various possible answers. Ask students to re-read the *Reminders* on page 122 before they begin the exam practice task.

WRITING PRACTICE

- **Structuring an argument (example answer)**
  Exercise 12, page 246

Focus on speaking 2 *Teachers and students (p.124)*

1 Read through the *Exam Briefing*, stressing the key components of a good performance. Then give students time to look through responses A–D individually and discuss them in pairs.

2 It would be useful to practise this *Useful language* as a whole-class activity. Suggest a mini topic, e.g. *How important is healthy eating?* and invite students to give an opinion. Try to get different responses using all four of the patterns if possible. Other possible mini topics: *Does travel broaden the mind? Is there too much interest in celebrities these days? Do you believe in global warming?*

3 These three expressions can be used in quite a wide range of ways, so it's a good idea to focus on each in turn and make sure students know some of the key grammatical pattern(s) which can follow, e.g.

- **It depends what kind of ... /what you mean by** ... + noun/noun phrase, e.g. *It depends what you mean by the word 'rewarding'.*
- **It depends if/whether** ... + clause, e.g. *It depends ... the conditions are right.*
- **It depends on** ... + noun/noun phrase, e.g. *It depends ... the weather; ... what it costs.*
- **In the past/I remember when** ... + past tense/*used to* (see page 115).
- **Some people think** (that) ... + clause, e.g. ... *Some people think the rules don't apply to them.*

Draw students' attention to *but* as a way of disagreeing with an opinion, and also remind them of the use of *while/whereas*. (See *Useful language*, page 123.)

Have a class discussion of the topic and encourage students to use as many examples of the target language as possible.

4 Arrange students in pairs and ask them to discuss as many of the topics as time allows. Monitor their work and give appropriate feedback.

Focus on writing 2 *Interpreting data (p.125)*

This task focuses on the importance of selecting key information from a detailed diagram. It also looks at ways of varying the expressions used in a description to avoid too much repetition.

1/2 Ask students to read through the *Reminders* and then study the exam task and bar chart.

Before they do the task, establish that it's neither appropriate nor possible to describe all the information in the diagram in 150 words. Ask what the main points of interest are, i.e. students' general strengths and weaknesses across subjects, and also any significant differences of performance by boys and girls in individual subjects.

3 Remind students that using your own words to express information from a diagram is likely to get a better score Before students tackle the exam task, you may also want to revise ways of reporting statistics and rounding up to the nearest figure (page 81) and possibly some of the comparative expressions from *Key Language* Exercise 7, page 214.

NB There is a gapped model answer for this task.

WRITING PRACTICE

- **Describing data (guided practice)**
  Exercise 13, page 247

Unit 12 Key

Lead-in *(p.118)*

1 **School (S):** headmaster, class, pupil, uniform, lesson, homework, secondary, teacher
College/University (U): professor, degree, lecturer, undergraduate, research, tutorial, seminar, fresher, doctorate, campus

2 **1 a)** one of (usually) three periods into which the school or university year is divided, especially in Britain
b) one of (usually) two periods into which the university year is divided, especially in the US and Australia
2 a) a section of a university or other large organisation, dealing with a particular subject or subjects, e.g. Department of Maths and Science
b) a group of related departments in a college or university, e.g. Faculty of Arts
Also all the lecturers in a particular faculty.
3 a) short piece of writing about a particular subject that you do as part of a course of study
b) a long piece of writing about a particular subject that you do as part of an advanced university degree

3 **A** pupil, lesson, homework, fresher, teacher, campus, essay, thesis (not degree or research oO)
B headmaster, professor, department
C uniform, lecturer, seminar, doctorate, secondary, faculty

Focus on listening 1 *(p.120)*

1 See Student's Book page 254.
2 1, 2 B, E (in any order) **3** familiar **4** tense and/or anxious/feeling/tense/anxious **5** full attention
6 to make notes **7** your judgement **8** feeling
9 win (an) argument **10** is not saying/does not say

Focus on listening 2 *(p.121)*

1 **1** one
2 The other words in the list: i.e. each is a single verb. You might also notice that the heading gives the first letter of each answer, so 3 will begin with the letter P, and 4 will begin with the letter S.
3 5 preposition; 6 verb (infinitive without *to* after modal auxiliary); 7 verb (-*ing* form after preposition); 8 verb (infinitive without *to*); 9 verb (could be present or present perfect, affirmative or negative)
4 three
5 Group kept in luxury
2 **1** Storage **2** Verbal **3** Preview **4** State
5 through it quickly **6** review the contents
7 paying attention **8** make (any) mistakes
9 know well **10** A

Focus on writing 1 *(p.122)*

4 **1** In an **evidence-led** approach, you only state your overall conclusion at the end, after evaluating all the evidence. In a **thesis-led** approach, you begin by stating your point of view and then set out reasons to justify this.
2 a **thesis-led** approach
3 an **evidence-led** approach
6 **1** *despite/in spite of* are followed by a noun group; *although* is followed by a subordinate clause.
2 *however, nevertheless, on the other hand*
3 *on the other hand*
7 (*Example answers*)
1 **Despite the fact that** football hooligans receive a lot of publicity, there are millions of spectators who cause no trouble at all.
2 **While** many people feel that censorship is unacceptable in a free society, it's undeniable that children need some form of protection from *unsuitable subject matter.*

3 Although medical advances are extending the human lifespan, not everyone wants *to live to be 100.*

4 Smoking is known to cause *lung cancer and other serious diseases.* **Nevertheless**, people have the right to *make their own health decisions.*

5 City life undoubtedly has many advantages such as *convenient shopping and leisure facilities.* **On the other hand**, city dwellers face many problems, including *crime and pollution.*

8 (*Example answers*)
1 <u>While/Although</u> the economy is improving …
2 Despite <u>the fact that/Even though</u> I agree …
3 … in spite <u>of</u> the fact …
4 Although modern vaccines … ~~but~~ …

Focus on speaking 2 *Teachers and students (p.124)*

1 (*Example answer*)
C Because it provides a full, well-balanced response. The ideas are well-linked and there is a good variety of grammatical structures and vocabulary. By comparison, A is a one-word answer giving the examiner no evidence of the candidate's ability; B is a full answer giving clear reasons for an opinion with well-linked ideas but this is a very personal (subjective) viewpoint. It's a good idea to try and be objective if possible, as in answer C; D has good ideas but is expressed in very simple sentences with no linking.

Focus on writing 2 *(p.125)*

2 1 English, Mathematics and sciences
2 Mathematics, sciences, Geography, History
3 English (65.2%, well over half)
4 English and French (The girls' pass rate in French was over/more than 50% higher than the boys').
5 Geography

3 1 get poor results **2** almost double **3** do well
4 percentage of successful candidates **5** figure
6 much **7** equal **8** roughly

Exam Practice
See *Writing Practice* Exercise 13, page 247.

Critical Thinking 3 *(p.127)*

Useful vocabulary: engage with; aspect, flaw,

In order to reinforce the message of this section it's important to take time to lead into the text and to discuss the pre- and post-reading questions in detail.

1 Give students no more than a minute to look at the headline and first couple of lines. Then ask them to close their books and open a class discussion about the likely topic of the article, and agree an answer, e.g. The use of the internet as a tool for learning, before continuing. Encourage students to suggest as many ideas as possible for the content of the article, without accepting or rejecting any at this stage.

2 When students have completed exercise 2, discuss their ideas and experiences.

Example answers:

2 The internet has enormous educational potential but because much of the information currently available is unreliable, it is only of limited value as a learning tool at present.

4 The author mentions finding some errors in the information about a particular quotation he was researching. This is only one piece of evidence and the problems are fairly minor, so the evidence is not very strong. The argument would benefit from more examples of preferably more serious inaccuracies found on the internet.

This is an interesting text with a high proportion of *Academic Word List* words in it. If you have time, you may want to take the opportunity for students to study it in more detail. To practise working out meaning from context, ask them to explain: *immersion learning* (para 1) and *a transcription error* (3).

You could also focus on vocabulary including: (teacher–pupil) engagement (para 1); to address (a problem) (2); chief (adj) (2); telling (adj) (3); to trace* (3); to cite* (3); to attribute* (3); to endorse (4); to censor (4); a boon (4) (* = *Academic Word List* items)

13 ▶ Bones to phones

To set the ball rolling ...

As a brief introduction, ask students to jot down all the ways they have communicated, apart from speaking, in the last 24 hours. Encourage them if necessary to extend the basic list of notes, email, etc. to include facial expression, gesture and even sounds (sighs, groans, laughs, etc.).

Lead-in *(p.128)*

1 This task encourages students to consider communications in broad terms and to think about some basic distinctions between various (mainly visual) systems. For interest, approximate dates of invention are included in the Key.

The task can be done fairly quickly, but if students are interested, and time allows, you could usefully develop the topic discussion to include some of the points below. This works well if you can prepare an OHP transparency or a PowerPoint slide of items A–H.

NB There are two basic types of writing system: *phonological* (representing sounds) – the majority of those used today – and *non-phonological* – as used in the earliest writing systems. Non-phonological symbols range from recognisable representations of objects (*pictograms*) as in C, to more abstract symbols standing for words, as in G. You could mention that the Chinese character for 'man' written three times stands for group, while 'woman' written twice stands for 'quarrel'!

2 To give the discussion more focus, ask students to try and agree on their answers. Make sure they justify their answers to **b**.

Focus on reading 1
Communication devices *(p.129)*

1 Give students time to read the texts and discuss ideas together. If need be, point out a few clues, e.g. **A** *digital networks, fashion accessory*; **B** *began to be worn, Switzerland*; **D** *send and receive pictures, office use*. When checking, ask students to say which information helped them. You could also ask students to imagine they could only have one of the five inventions, and say which they would choose, and why.

2 For greater clarity, introduce each type of participle clause and its meaning on the board first. It may be helpful to point out that the term *-ed* in *-ed* clauses refers to all past participles, whether they end in *-ed* or not. Perfect participles, e.g. *Having remained*, may need special attention – make sure students realise they are *-ing* (rather than *-ed*) forms.

3/4 This is an important language area, which should be reinforced regularly by asking students to identify participle clauses in reading texts.

NB *Key Language* Exercise 24 provides practice in using the most common verbs in participle clauses.

KEY LANGUAGE

- **Common verbs in *-ed* and *-ing* clauses**
  Exercise 24, page 228

Focus on reading 2 *Bones to phones (p.130)*

1 Before they begin, ask students to read the heading and introduction to the reading text (*Radio survived ...*) and briefly speculate about the content of the article.

2 Read through the *Exam Briefing* and *Task Approach* and then focus on the example. Identify the key word (*where ...*) then ask students to find matching information in paragraph C (*... is housed on the internet*). Let them underline key words and phrases in the remaining questions and follow the recommended *Task Approach*. When checking answers, make sure students can justify their answers by reference to the text.

3 Ask students to begin by underlining or highlighting in the text the eight media listed in the box, so they are easy to locate. Again, use the example as a way of reviewing this task-type. Ask students to read about missile mail in the text (para E) and pinpoint the information which matches the description (*Before man reaches the Moon, ... guided missile*).

They should then underline key words or phrases in the remaining questions before studying the information about each medium in the text, and completing the task.

4 Elicit the three key questions from the *Task Approach* on page 52. (Is it mentioned in the text? Is it true? Is it relevant?) When checking, make sure students can justify their answers by reference to the text where possible.

Focus on vocabulary *Introducing examples (p.134)*

The expressions are not interchangeable, so check that students are clear about when to use each one, and draw their attention to relevant punctuation features. If you have time, you may want to explore this language area in more depth, by looking at common collocations, e.g. *X is a good/typical/striking/example of Y*, or by adding extra expressions, e.g. *... a (good) case in point.*

NB If you have time for more vocabulary study, you could also focus on the use of the verb *doubt*, which occurs in the text, and set the *Key Language* exercise below for class or homework.

KEY LANGUAGE
• **The verb *doubt***   Exercise 25, page 228

Focus on speaking *Comparing and contrasting (p.134)*

1 Let students study the pictures and establish the three methods of communication (email, texting, writing a letter). Have a whole class discussion, using the students' own experience of these media as far as possible. (See Key for suggestions.) To provide greater focus, ask them which they would use for specific purposes, such as breaking up with a boy/girlfriend, applying for a job, arranging a party at short notice, closing a bank account, keeping in touch with friends abroad.

2 To set the ball rolling, discuss a few extra notes which could be added under *letter*, e.g. *slow, delayed feedback, pictures/documents can be enclosed*). Give students time to complete the mindplan, monitoring their work to check for spelling or other mistakes. Afterwards have a round-up of ideas, so that everyone can add to their notes.

3 Before the exam practice, focus on the *Useful language*. You could give additional practice if necessary by asking students to compare different methods of travel (private car/taxi/train/plane, etc.). You might also want to rehearse a few ways of expressing personal preferences, e.g. *I much prefer using the telephone to writing a letter*.

Unit 13 Key

Lead-in (p.128)

1 A Sign language (1775, France) – hand movements representing letters or words

B Morse code (1837, USA) – groups of long or short sounds representing a letter

C Egyptian hieroglyphics (c. 3000 BC) – picture signs indicating words

D symbols indicating washing instructions (modern)

E Shorthand (Pitmanscript, 1837) – a system of speedwriting

F Hindi script – each letter representing a sound, as in English

G Chinese characters (c. 1700 BC) – abstract symbols representing words

H mathematical symbols

1 Morse code (not a written medium). Other answers are possible.

2 They both represent recognisable pictures of things in the world.

3 (*Example answer*) Road signs

2 a 1 Calendar **2** Mechanical clock **3** Printing press **4** Telephone **5** X-rays **6** Television **7** Satellite

Focus on reading 1 (p.129)

1 See Student's Book, page 254.

3 -ing clauses

A *making them far more convenient to use* (which made them …);

C *replacing papyrus rolls* (when it replaced …); *being both portable* (as it was both …); *Having remained dominant* (It has remained dominant … but may now …)

E *Having originated* … (It originated …. and (then) evolved …)

-ed clauses

B *Invented in Germany* … (This useful gadget was invented in Germany and (it) became …); *At first regarded purely as* … (At first it was purely regarded as … but it began …)

E *technology developed* …. (technology which was/ had been developed …); *Initially used only by scientists* … (Initially it was used only by scientists but it was (then) released …)

4 (*Example answers*)

1 He produced an essay *based* on information *downloaded* from the internet.

2 The paper *containing* the results of the survey is about to be published.

3 The damage *caused* by the flood will take years to be repaired.

4 *Having finished* his speech, the President answered reporters' questions.

5 *Realising/Having realised* that he had lost the confidence of his team, the manager resigned.

Focus on reading 2 (p.130)

2 1 C (*Example*) *housed on the internet*

2 G (quipu) *did not survive long/were burnt*

3 E *did not lead to a postal revolution*

4 A (bone-notching) *still a mystery; used for so long – about 90,000 years*

5 D (lukasa) *were used to teach traditional lore …*

6 B *The only criteria are …*

7 H *another feature of long-lasting media: they tend to be simple*

8 F *a close association with some form of power in society*

3 9 C (para E) *many cities boasted … made up of underground pipes.*

10 B (D) *By learning the shapes … and the sequences in which they appeared.*

11 E (F) *These knots were tied by an official class … historians, scribes and accountants.*

12 A (A) *… present thinking is that … lunar calendar.*

13 F (H) *These attempts may vary … all based on the same simple idea.*

4 14 B (paragraph C) *Sterling and Kadrey set the ball rolling, but ultimately it is a communal effort …*

15 D (G) quipu *could have been taken a great deal further*

Focus on vocabulary (p.134)

1 1 Take, for example, …

2 In the category … one group stands out …

3 … illustrate the point.

4 … to name but a few.

2 (*Example answers*)

1 The fact that many older people have no idea how to download music **illustrates this point**.

2 Among these, **one** in particular **stands out**: the high costs of calls.

3 **Take, for example,** the dishwasher, which takes time to load and unload.

4 It is thought that they may not develop normal social skills, **for example**.

5 … the last hundred years, computers, lasers and fibre optics, **to name but a few**.

Focus on speaking (p.134)

1 Possible factors include:

speed, e.g. 'snail' mail vs email

cost, e.g. postage vs cost of mobile phone contract

feedback, e.g. instant or delayed

other: How secure? Is there a written record? Can you send words and pictures?

14 ▶ The proper channels

To set the ball rolling ...

You could begin by doing an informal class survey to find out a bit about students' own preferences with regard to various media. For speed, use the Media survey (questions 7–10) on page 140 as the basis for mini interviews. Point out the need to formulate suitable questions, and practise if necessary beforehand. Alternatively, devise a fuller questionnaire for discussion in pairs. Afterwards, ask a few students to report back on what their partner said.

Lead-in (p.138)

1 The example illustrates two typical features of text messaging: the shortening of words, usually by leaving out vowels (MN = MAN, TCH = TEACH, etc.) and the use of numbers which sound like words (4 = *for*, 2 = *to*, etc.). If students are struggling to interpret the quote, ask them to try saying the first few 'words' aloud.

2 a These examples introduce an additional feature of text messaging: the use of letters which sound like words or parts of words (U = *you*, C = *see*, etc.).

b Students will probably be familiar with the symbols shown here, though perhaps not with the term (a combination of *emotion* + *icon*). Ask why emoticons are needed in email and other electronic messages, and establish that they are used to express humour or emotion where a message might otherwise be misinterpreted in the absence of vocal or facial expression.

After the exercise, you could find out if students are familiar with any other styles of emoticon. For example, there is a style popular in East Asia which can be understood without tilting your head to the left, e.g. (*_*). You could mention that studies at universities in Japan and the UK, show that Japanese and other East Asians read facial expressions by looking mainly at the eyes, and the researchers noted that this is reflected in East Asian emoticons which put emphasis on the eyes, compared to Western emoticons which focus mainly on the mouth. Compare the Japanese emoticon for a sad face ; _ ; with the Western equivalent : (.

NB There is an article on the subject, which you could use for further discussion, at: http://www.livescience.com/health/070510_facial_culture.html

3 You could help by telling students that four words have no silent letters. Let them compare answers before checking. Practise orally.

4 Practise the three sounds with more examples if necessary. To cater for varieties of English such as American English, you will need to include a fourth sound /aə/, as in *hat*. Explain that this sound usually replaces the British /ɒː/ in American English (though not in words with an *r* after the vowel, e.g. *hard, far, start*).

Again, you could help by telling students there should be six words in each column. Let students compare answers and practise orally after checking.

Focus on speaking 1
Communication problems (p.139)

If you have time, introduce this section (with books closed) by writing the following newspaper headlines on the board or overhead projector. Ask students to speculate about the story behind each headline, encouraging them to use appropriate language for speculation, e.g. *I think it might/could be about … It must be to do with …,* etc. NB The headlines match extracts C, A, D and B respectively.

Information stress and email overload

Students love social networking sites and so do employers

Emails spell disaster for English teaching

When lessons interrupt an important call

1 Set a strict time limit for reading to encourage skimming and then let students discuss answers in pairs. You could usefully check some of the language in the extracts afterwards, e.g. A *vet, turned down*; B *fads, undermine, hence*; C *cope, instantaneous*; D *concise, missives*.

2 These are fairly meaty topics, which should provide plenty of scope for discussion practice. Monitor the pairwork and make sure students are considering various aspects of the subject and using a good range of language.

Focus on listening 1 Media
survey (p.140)

If you didn't use the survey at the *Lead-in* stage, give students a few moments to study the questions. Afterwards, you might want to focus on a few useful or interesting expressions from the recording script, e.g. *many happy returns, I'm not terribly up on …, (it) bores me stiff, make a point of* (doing something), *(it) leaves me cold* (an informal expression).

Focus on listening 2 *Couch potatoes (p.141)*

Read through the *Task Approach* and then study the diagrams in questions 1–4. Encourage students to 'read' these quickly by asking focus questions about key features (see below). Ask them to make further sentences about the data and emphasise how helpful this is in tuning them in to the recording they are about to hear.

- What does the bar chart show: a current comparison or changes over time? What does each bar represent? What measurement is used? What is the highest percentage of viewers in any country? etc.
- What do the pie charts show: a current comparison or changes over time? What do the three colours represent? What measurement is likely to be used? (fractions, e.g. *a third*, or percentages, e.g. *about 25%*). Which diagram shows the largest proportion of news/ factual material? etc.
- What do the graphs show: a current comparison or changes over time? What measurement is used? What do the coloured lines represent? Which diagram shows …, etc.

Afterwards, you might want to focus on a few useful or interesting expressions from the recording script, e.g. *a heavy viewer*, *to account for*, *news stroke* (= the oblique or slash sign */) factual*, *an interesting angle* (on a subject), *to be/feel left out*, *to be old hat* (= familiar, old-fashioned, unexciting).

Focus on writing 1 *Dealing with different data (p.142)*

NB It's very important that students take note of the information in the *Exam Briefing* on the weighting of each part in the Writing paper. In the exam, it's all too easy to get bogged down in Task 1 and find yourself short of time to complete Task 2, which is worth more marks.

This is quite a complex task and it's worth spending class time in preparation. Use focus questions to draw students' attention to significant features and also revise useful language.

- What is the focus of each graph? (world news and local news)
- What are the main parameters? (percentage of people, time scale, media)
- Is there any difference in the ranking of the three media in the two graphs? (TV is the most popular source of world news; newspapers are **marginally**

more popular than television for local news.)
- What is significant about the first graph? (Television is **by far the most popular** medium for world news; there has been **little change** in the relative popularity of the media over the period.)
- What is significant about the second graph? (There has been **a significant decline** in the popularity of newspapers and **a corresponding increase** in the popularity of television.)
- Describe this increase. (The percentage has **almost doubled**; popularity has **risen** from 19% in 1987 to 37% in 1997).
- Compare the popularity of radio for world and local news, etc.

NB If students are having difficulty in selecting significant data in this kind of task, you could also prepare a set of sentences describing aspects of the graph and ask which should be included, which not (and why).

Focus on speaking 2 *The written word (p.144)*

Additional discussion topics
- (Pairs) Ask students to list as many reasons for using for the internet as possible, then discuss which they personally use the internet for most, and how they would feel if they had to manage without the internet for a month. You could then reveal the top six reasons, according to recent research:

  1 Use email
  2 Gather information
  3 Online banking
  4 Sharing photos, videos and files
  5 Geographic navigation services
  6 Shopping online

Interestingly, the research showed that young people aged 13–18 primarily use the internet for different reasons, including downloading music, playing games online, blogging, and social networking.

- (Pairs/groups) Write a number of topics on slips of paper and give a set to each pair/group face down. Students should turn up one topic at a time and discuss for 2–3 minutes.

  Example topics:
  - What are the pros and cons of internet shopping?
  - Should governments censor the internet?
  - Is it important for schools to have internet access? Why?
  - True or False? It's no longer necessary to write letters.

Focus on writing 2 *Beginning and ending (p.144)*

If necessary, revise the difference between the two approaches to essay structure, **evidence-led** (page 65) and **thesis-led** (page 122), before you begin. The exercises can be done either in pairs or as a class, but it would be useful to finish off with a round-up of key points.

Unit 14 Key

Lead-in *(p.138)*

1 Give a man a fish and you feed him for a day. Teach a man to fish and you feed him for a lifetime.

2 a 1 through 2 tomorrow 3 for ever
4 Are you there? 5 See you later
6 By the way 7 Thank you 8 Cool
  b 1 happy face: used when giving/receiving good news
2 frown: bad news coming
3 winking face: used when joking
4 sceptical face
5 shocked face

3 a through; gh
  b an<u>sw</u>er comba<u>t</u> ✓ i<u>s</u>land mus<u>cle</u>
behin<u>d</u> ✓ dou<u>bt</u> <u>i</u>gnorant ✓ <u>p</u>sychologist
ca<u>l</u>m golfe<u>r</u> ✓ <u>k</u>nife recei<u>p</u>t
clim<u>b</u> ha<u>lf</u> lis<u>t</u>en <u>w</u>rist

4 /ɑː/ calm, class, command, drama, half, past
/ɑ/ quality, quantity, swallow, wander, watch, what
/ɔː/ fall, law, raw, walk, warn, water

Focus on speaking 1 *(p.139)*

1 1 **A** internet/social networking websites **B** mobile phones **C** emails **D** text-messaging and emails
2 (*Example answers*)
  A The way information on social networking sites can be used by potential employers **B** The problems of children using mobile phones in school **C** The stress which can be caused by emails **D** Teachers' concerns about the effect of text-messaging and emailing on spelling

Focus on listening 1 *(p.140)*

1 Matthews **2** 21 **3** full-time student **4** sports
5 (national) news **6** TV reviews **7** C **8** B
9 B **10** A

Focus on listening 2 *(p.141)*

1 B **2** D **3** C **4** B **5** B **6** C **7** A **8–10** A, D, F (in any order)

Focus on writing 2 *(p.144)*

2 1 B 2 C 3 A
3 B
4 1 B 2 A 3 C

Reflective Learning 4 *(p.147)*

Useful vocabulary: interchange(ably), proofreading, eliminate

1 Let students work through the questions in pairs and then discuss the issues as a class (see notes in the Students Book page 259).

Additional note:

In a study of over 2,000 scientists throughout history, it was found that the most respected figures produced many 'bad' ideas as well as great ones. In other words, they weren't afraid to fail or to produce substandard work on the way to achieving excellence.

2 Depending on your students' ability, you may need to look in detail at the types of mistake and illustrate each one before they do exercise 2.

3 Look through the *Ideas for dealing with errors* and invite students to suggest a few of their own 'favourite' mistakes. Discuss various ways of revising a problem area of language

4/5 Monitor the 'favourite' mistakes that students list, advising as necessary. If any of these appear regularly, you might want to plan some remedial teaching. Ask students to report back on their progress towards the vocabulary learning goal they set for *Reflective Learning 3*. Emphasise the positive and focus on any success, however small. Offer advice and encouragement as necessary.

Key: See Student's Book, page 259.

15 ▶ Beyond gravity

To set the ball rolling ...

Use the photographs on pages 148/149 (or any other suitable picture on a space exploration theme) as the focus for a brief preliminary chat, to gauge students' interest and knowledge, and elicit some topic vocabulary. Try to steer clear of topics included in the *Lead-in* quiz, but if they should arise, avoid specific details.

Notes on photographs

page 148: the International Space Station against the blackness of space, as seen from the Space Shuttle *Discovery* as the two spacecraft begin their undocking (separation) process. Crews had earlier completed nine days of maintenance work aboard the shuttle and station. 25 March, 2009

page 149: Anousheh Ansari, the first female private space explorer and the first astronaut of Iranian descent. In September 2006 she undertook an eight-day expedition aboard the International Space Station as part of the crew of the Soyuz TMA-9. While in space, she wrote a blog describing the experience of lift-off, talking about the sights and smells of the space station, and explaining how everyday activities such as eating and washing up worked in zero gravity.

Lead-in *(p.148)*

This warm-up activity allows students to share their knowledge of a few milestones in the Space Age and to speculate about some possibly surprising statistics. It also provides some background information for the Speaking topics which follow, and for the optional writing task.

Focus on speaking 1 *The final frontier (p.149)*

1 Let students read through the extracts and discuss briefly. You could ask: **A** *Who is Sir Richard Branson and what is the likely motive behind his 'dream'?* (A successful entrepreneur, the owner of Virgin brand of companies, which includes the airline Virgin Atlantic. As a businessman, his motive must at least in part be profit); **B** *Who is asking the 'big question'?* (Probably a journalist or other commentator); **D** *What effect did her experience of space tourism have on Anousheh Ansari?* etc.

Clarify vocabulary as necessary, e.g. **A** *accessible*, **B** *manned*, **D** *sheer*, *perspective*.

2 Focus first on the *Useful language* and practise by firing a few challenging questions at students. Encourage them to make the most of the discussion points by giving detailed reasons for their opinions, and monitor their conversations for any language that might need attention.

Invite brief feedback afterwards and perhaps develop question 4 into a whole-class discussion. You could record some of the arguments on the board, as the basis for an optional writing task on this topic.

You could also check other topic vocabulary as a link to the two reading texts in the unit, e.g. *astronaut* (*cosmonaut* in the former Soviet Union) *space mission*, *spacecraft*, *space suit*, *weightlessness* and *(zero) gravity*, etc.

Optional additional discussion points
1 In what ways would the world be different if there were no satellites in orbit around the Earth?
2 How realistic is the idea of human beings escaping to another planet if the Earth were to become uninhabitable?
3 What are the chances of finding intelligent life on another planet?

Focus on reading 1 *Out of this world (p.150)*

1 Give students a few minutes for this task and then let them compare ideas with a partner. If you discuss these as a class, avoid confirming or denying any suggestions at this stage. Draw their attention to the *Glossary* after the text and point out that this way of explaining difficult or technical words is also an exam feature.

2–4 With less able students it would be useful to read through the *Reminders* as a class, returning to the original *Task Approach* if necessary. Highlighting key words in the questions is such an important part of the recommended strategy for all three exam tasks that it is worth allotting time for this and checking results as a class. When checking, make sure students justify their answers by reference to specific wording in the text.

2 Ask which reading skill is required for this task (scanning). Remind students about time pressure in the exam and the importance of reading as efficiently as possible. Give them a time check after 5 minutes and tell them that's about all they should allow for this task in the exam.

3 See if students can remember the key points about this task. Ask:

- How is a Yes/No/NG task (as here) different from a True/False/NG task? (The first focuses on the writer's opinion while the second focuses on facts.)
- Are the questions in passage order? (Yes)
- When should you write True or Yes? (When a statement exactly matches information in the text)
- When should you write False or No? (When a statement says the opposite to information in the text)
- What if statement seems true but there's no information in the text? (Write Not Given)
- What's the first step to tackling this task? (Study the questions and underline key words or phrases)

4 This task was introduced on page 32. Remind students that questions are <u>not</u> in passage order. With weaker students you may want to let them work together to locate and underline experts, and also to underline key words in the questions before they continue.

Focus on speaking 2 *Sci-fi* (p.152)

This task can be used for either informal or formal exam practice, depending on your students' degree of readiness. In either case, check that everyone is absolutely clear about the procedure first. Ask them to explain this and to mention any advice they can remember. Recap the general advice in the *Exam Briefing* on page 61 (and also the *Exam Tip* there) if necessary.

Focus on reading 2 *Surviving in space* (p.152)

With books closed, ask students to guess how long they think a journey to Mars will take. Then refer them to the diagram on page 153 (972 days).

1 Ask them to cover the text, leaving just the headline and subheading visible and then discuss possible health risks in pairs. Invite brief feedback, and jot ideas on the board.

2 Set an appropriate time for skimming/scanning (say 5 minutes) and stick to it, to discourage intensive reading at this stage. Check results and compare with students' predictions.

3 Unless your students are at or near exam standard, allow a little time for them to find their bearings in this quite long text. Elicit ways of forming a general picture of the content, e.g. by **sampling** the text and/ or by **skim-reading** and circling key topics in each paragraph. Make sure they study the *Reminders*, and if any students are struggling with particular

questions, you may want to direct them to relevant areas of the text. Allow time for them to compare answers before checking.

For the True/False/Not Given section, review the distinction between False and Not Given answers if necessary, and use the checking phase to establish the difference very clearly. If students have had problems with question 5, make a teaching point of the difference between *few* and *a few*, *little* and *a little* (*Error Hit List*, page 166).

When checking the multiple-choice section, ask students to provide evidence from the text for their answers. Those who choose option B have failed to distinguish between long and short space flights, and this provides an opportunity to underline the importance of grasping the main issues in a text and reading the options very carefully.

Although the diagrams may look complicated, the task is straightforward once the relevant section of text has been found. This is where the initial text sampling or skimming that students have done should prove invaluable.

When matching opinions to experts, it may be helpful to work together to identify key phrases in one or two of the opinions and to ask for suggestions as to parallel expressions, e.g. 12: *prevent many deaths* = save many lives). Again, ask students to say which words/phrases in the text match the opinions.

NB The text contains a number of informal expressions which you could focus on if time allows, e.g.

no worse for wear (also *none the worse for wear*) (line 15) = unharmed by an experience.
Compare: *He looked a bit the worse for wear after his all-night journey.* = in a poor condition because of an experience.

an unknown realm (17–18) = unexplored territory. NB *realm* can also mean an area of activity, interest or study.

mere hiccups (61) = comparatively small problems.

NB literally, a *hiccup* is a sharp repeated sound made in the throat, especially after eating or drinking.

bear fruit (87) = have a successful result.

NB The text also provides an opportunity to focus on two important areas of language: noun formation and *-ing* forms and infinitives.

KEY LANGUAGE
• **Word building: nouns** Exercise 27, page 229
• ***-ing* forms vs infinitives** Exercise 28, page 230

Unit 15 Key

Lead-in *(p.148)*

See Student's Book, page 254.

Additional note

5 $10 million was the cost for each launch of the *Pegasus*. $300 million is the cost of a space-shuttle mission on a Low Earth Orbit.

Focus on reading 1 *(p.150)*

2 1 $100 million per person (line 6)
  2 110 km (15–16)
  3 climate change (36–38)
  4 Gaia theory (46–47)

3 5 N ... *since then others have followed* (line 5)
  6 NG
  7 Y ... *1.5 tonnes "seems low for taking someone into space"* (32/3)
  8 N ... *in a well-judged PR exercise* ... (42)
  9 Y ... *Or would it be better ...good works.* (69–70)

4 10 E (57–62)
  11 D (47–51)
  12 B (23–26)

Focus on reading 2 *(p.152)*

3 1 F ... *more than two-thirds* (line 1)
  2 T ... *may gain five centimetres* (12–13)
  3 NG This may be true, but it's not mentioned in the text.
  4 T ... *polyethylene shielding will absorb the radiation* (64–65)
  5 F Stress is caused when people have *few tasks* (78) and *little to do* (81). (See *Error Hit List*, page 166.)
  6–8 (in any order) A (e.g. lines 50–53) C (34–37) F e.g. with drugs (48–50); by making body parts (53–57)
  9 coronal mass ejections
  10 electrically charged gas
  11 cosmic rays
  12 E *This technology has the potential to save ... lives* (99–101)
  13 A *These changes are the price of a ticket to space.* (22–23)
  14 F *The more research that's done ... everyone is going to be.* (111–113)

16 ▶ Going forward

To set the ball rolling ...

Ask students to look at the title of the unit and read the definition, then mention that this is a very current idiom, often heard in interviews with businessmen and politicians. Point out that grammatically it is a fixed phrase, which cannot be conjugated.

For speed, with books closed, write prediction B from the *Lead-in* on the board, and ask students to guess who the speaker was, and say why this prediction was ill-advised. Ask for examples of everyday predictions, e.g. weather forecasts, political polls, predicted exam grades in school reports, star signs (if appropriate), and introduce a brief discussion of students' opinions as to the value (or otherwise) of such predictions.

Lead-in *(p.158)*

1 Ask students to work in pairs to answer questions 1 and 2. Encourage them to say as much as they can about each subject, e.g. why Albert Einstein was very far from a failure, why prediction C was badly timed. In feedback, include some of the points from the Discussion notes and Example answer in the Key.

> **Optional language input**
>
> If you feel your students have a reasonable grasp of the basic tenses, and could handle an extra one without suffering overload, you could introduce the following language, known as the future in the past:
> *The captain thought the voyage **was going to be** uneventful.*
> *They didn't realise that Einstein **would** one day win the Nobel Prize for Physics.*
>
> This language is used to talk about something that people in the past expected to happen in the future. Whether it actually happened later or not is not important. There are two forms, *was/were going to* and *would*. Encourage students to use this language to talk about each prediction.

2 Give students time to study the illustrations and discuss ideas. Clarify vocabulary as necessary, e.g. *sawdust* (very small pieces of wood which are left after cutting wood), *solar range* (a cooker which uses the power of the sun), *hose* (a long rubber tube typically used for directing water on to fires or gardens, as illustrated), *aero car* (a 'flying car', i.e. an aircraft which can also drive on roads, designed in 1949 but never produced).

Afterwards, open up a class discussion. Ask students to focus on B, D and E, and describe the differences between the prediction and the modern day reality (see notes in the Key).

As the illustrations represent visual predictions, there is a further opportunity to use the language of the future in the past (see *Optional language input*), e.g. *People didn't know the internet was going to be invented. They thought everyone would have a private plane.*

Focus on speaking 1 *Predicting the future (p.159)*

1 Give students time to read through the predictions and check any unknown vocabulary before they begin. Make sure they are working together to discuss and categorise the issues, according to the instructions. Afterwards, discuss students' results and reasons, but avoid definitive answers which would pre-empt the listening task to follow.

2 Organise this activity as pair interviews for more direct exam practice. Afterwards, invite brief feedback, and perhaps develop one or two questions into a whole-class discussion.

KEY LANGUAGE
• **Expressing probability** Exercise 30, page 232

Focus on listening 1 *Reality or science fiction? (p.160)*

For extra support, give students time to look through the questions and perhaps discuss ideas in pairs. You could also talk through their predicted answers before the listening phase. Ask students to compare answers before checking.

Focus on listening 2 *The techno-house (p.161)*

Read the advice in the *Reminders*, and let students study the diagram. Check their ideas and discuss topic vocabulary, as appropriate. For extra support, allow time for students to study the remaining questions, and perhaps discuss predicted answers. Ask them to compare answers before the checking phase.

Focus on writing 1 *Explaining how something works (p.162)*

1/2 Let students look briefly at the diagram on page 163 and explain that however complicated such a process may seem at first sight, it's usually fairly straightforward to describe as long as you study it carefully and follow the recommended *Task Approach*. Read through the *Task Approach* as a class.

Point out that when the topic is a technical process (rather than a natural one), it's often helpful to start by describing the basic layout and function of the equipment. Read through the *Useful Language* as a class. Give a few examples to illustrate the meaning and use of the various expressions, e.g. *a candle* (a device for giving light/a device which you burn to give light. It consists of a wax cylinder which contains a piece of string called a wick).

NB It would also be useful to revise the expressions *looks (a bit) like …,* and *made of … .* from the *Useful language* on page 75.

If you feel students need some guided practice before they move on to exercises 1 and 2, give them a few more simple objects and/or systems to describe, e.g. *a saw, a dishwasher, TV remote control, bicycle, a parking meter, cash dispenser,* etc.

Exercises 1 and 2 can be done in pairs. Students would benefit from making a written record of some of the items, if time allows.

3 Check answers to questions 1–3, then ask students to say what the main purpose of the system is. Go through the process step by step, asking students to explain what happens at each point. This should be in their own words – they don't need to use the correct terminology or the words of the model answer. The important thing is that they understand how the system works.

4 When students have completed the task, check answers and look in more detail at how the model answer follows the *Task Approach* on page 162.

NB Explain that while concluding sentences are a useful feature they are not always necessary or possible, e.g. when the overview has already covered all the summary information that can be given (as in this case).

Focus on speaking 2 *Personal goals (p.164)*

1 If you can prepare an overhead transparency or a PowerPoint slide of the language of probability from *Key Language* Exercise 30, this will be a useful way of guiding the checking phase, and drawing students' attention to some of the key issues. Remind them to note down errors they make in correction so that these can be revised regularly and, hopefully, eliminated.

2 This is an important topic area for both Part 1 and Part 2 of the Interview. The activity gives students the opportunity to practise talking about a future goal and also to listen to fellow students' descriptions. If there is time, ask students to repeat the exercise with one or more different topics.

Refresh students' memories about preparing and using mindplans if necessary, using a separate topic, e.g. *A person you'd like to meet.*

Rearrange seating to facilitate group discussion (if possible), and check that students are clear about the instructions, have each chosen a different topic, and are equipped to keep time. Allow a couple of minutes for thinking/note-making.

Monitor students' performances, and note points for feedback. Afterwards, ask students to report back on what another group member said.

Use the feedback stage to identify key points of a successful long turn, e.g. covering both the *describe* and *explain* elements, and using a good range of language. Invite students to mention examples from their groupwork to illustrate these points.

Focus on writing 2 *Summarising sentences (p.165)*

1/2 Read through the introduction and *Useful language*, drawing students' attention to the more impersonal use of *we* rather than *I*. Students may find it easier to work in pairs to complete exercise 2.

2 This is quite a challenging task for weaker students. In this case, be prepared to give extra support in the form of prompts or possible answers to choose from. These are just suggestions:

we should look at the arguments against. (3)
Having considered the latest theories about teaching, (5)
the disadvantages. (1)
Having heard the evidence in favour of slowing drivers down, (6)
if this can be justified. (2)
Given some of the frightening experiences we have just heard about, (4)

3 Read through the *Reminders*, and revise the language on pages 83 and 84 if necessary. If students are still weak in this area of writing, have a planning phase in class, so you can discuss approaches and check paragraph plans, etc. You could also supply the following introduction:

The last hundred years have seen rapid and dramatic developments in many areas, including medicine, transport, …

With more able students, the topic would be suitable for timed exam practice.

WRITING PRACTICE

- **Presenting and justifying an opinion (example answer)**
  Exercise 15, page 248

Unit 16 Key

Lead-in (p.158)

1 1 (*Discussion notes*)

A Despite his poor school report, Albert Einstein's scientific work was to revolutionise physics in the 20th century. He was awarded the Nobel Prize for Physics in 1920.

B Despite the captain's faith in its supposedly unsinkable design, the passenger ship *Titanic* sank, with the loss of 1,513 lives.

C The first Moon landing took place just 12 years later in 1969.

D The first mass-produced personal computers were produced less than 20 years later, and computer ownership has been growing rapidly ever since.

E The telephone quickly proved to be a great success. Four years after its invention in 1876, there were 30,000 in use.

F The typewriter caught on quickly after its introduction and soon became indispensable in offices around the world, with portable typewriters for home use following.

G The first mass-produced car, the Oldsmobile, was produced a year later in 1901. It has been estimated that there are around 500 million cars in the world today (with one billion forecast for 2025).

2 (*Example answer*)

Predictions often extrapolate from the current situation, assuming that conditions will not change and technological development will imitate existing processes. In E–G, the assumption is that social conditions will remain stable. Cars will be restricted to the rich, who will employ chauffeurs to drive them. Labour will continue to be cheap, allowing companies to employ messenger boys, and communications will be local. None of these has proved to be correct.

2 (*Example answers*)

B Solar power is quite widely used nowadays to provide domestic lighting and heating but because it is entirely dependent on available sunlight, it is mainly used to provide an ancillary rather than a main energy source, especially in a country like the UK. Solar cookers exist but they are much simpler devices than the one shown. They use heat from the sun for cooking food outdoors. Because they cost nothing to run and use no fuel, they are promoted by humanitarian agencies as a way of slowing deforestation and also reducing fire risk.

D The 'picture phone' we use for shopping is, of course, the computer + internet.

E Private planes exist, but are so prohibitively expensive that only business corporations and the super-rich can afford them.

Notice that these predictions assume the continuation of traditional family roles with Father as breadwinner, Mother as housewife. It fails to foresee the more complex situations we have today where both parents may go out to work, and housework may be shared equally. It also fails to foresee the concept of a 'house husband', where a woman is the main breadwinner.

Focus on listening 1 (p.160)

1 social (and) economic   **2** technology
3 into existence   **4** (About) half/50% of (the) / (About) 3,000   **5** 4–6 (four to six) billion
6 more (and) smaller   **7** 2025   **8** political stability
9 Japan (and) Korea   **10** problem situations

Focus on listening 2 (p.161)

1 C *demand for the house of the future is still very low* (A – only in special show homes; B – the technology is *already in place*)

2 A *the thing they're mostly concerned about is location* (B – most prefer *a traditional-looking house*; C – … *not terribly interested in*)

3 B *a saving of twenty weeks on conventional construction* (A – *save both time and money*)

4 grass   **5** glasshouse   **6** pond   **7** solar energy
8 Internet House   **9** office or car   **10** staircase

Focus on writing 1 (p.162)

1 a) A burglar alarm is **a device** which makes a loud noise when someone tries to get into a building illegally.

b) Central heating is **a system** which **causes** warm air or water **to** circulate through pipes in order to heat a building.

c) A photocopier is **a machine** which **is used for** making photographic copies of documents.

2 a) An umbrella is **a device** which **prevents** people **from** getting wet when it rains. It consists of a folding circular folding frame which is covered in cloth.

b) A hammer is **a tool** which **is used for** hitting nails into wood. It consists of a heavy metal head attached to a long handle, which is usually made of wood.

c) Sat-nav is **a system** which **enables** drivers **to** find their way to a destination using information received from a satellite. It consists of a small box, which you fix to the dashboard of the car, and an electric lead which you plug into a suitable power source. The box has a screen and a number of controls.

3 1 evacuated evaporation chamber, turbine, condensing chamber

  2 1 kilometre

  3 desalinated water

4 1 for creating/producing/generating; which creates/produces/generates

  2 in temperature

  3 29 degrees

  4 a/1 kilometre

  5 consists of

  6 is connected to

  7 is heated

  8 (evacuated) evaporation chamber

  9 to turn/rotate

  10 After (leaving)

  11 enters/goes into

  12 (cold) seawater

  13 desalinated water

  14 is returned/returns

Focus on speaking 2 (p.164)

1 1 ✓ **2** … you will probably fail …

  3 … there's <u>a</u> 90% probability … **4** ✓ **5** ✓

  6 In my opinion/view **7** … a good/strong chance/a strong possibility … **8** ✓

  9 … unlikely <u>that</u> a new form of energy <u>will</u> be found … **10** ✓

Focus on writing 2 (p.165)

2 (*Example answers*)

  1 … the arguments in favour of co-educational schools.

  2 … whether this is a good use of public money.

  3 … we need to look at the counter-argument.

  4 Given the costs involved, …

  5 Having discussed some recent developments in teaching, …

  6 Having looked at some of the arguments for reducing speed on our roads, …

Critical Thinking 4 (p.167)

Useful vocabulary: emphasise/emphasis; minimum/minimise; maximum/maximise

1 Look at the example and ask students to put their finger over the word *interestingly*. Then ask what this adverb adds to the meaning. (The writer considers this fact worth thinking about.) Discuss a few more examples in the same way.

*West Nile disease has spread **surprisingly** quickly this year.* (The writer considers that this was faster than might have been expected.)

*Third world debt remains **worryingly** high.* (The writer thinks this is a matter of concern.)

***Predictably**, computer sales have slowed during the recession.* (The writer thinks this is exactly as might have been expected.)

After exercise 1, let students compare answers in pairs and clarify meanings and use as necessary.

2 Again, it would be useful to give more examples to check meanings and illustrate the two patterns before students do the exercise.

*Why is it so **significant that** water was found on the Moon?*

*It's **difficult to** understand how an expert could make such an elementary mistake.*

*It is **disappointing that** the country has not reduced its greenhouse emissions./It's **disappointing to** report that the country …*

3/4 Look at the examples and make sure students are clear about the two kind of emphasisers and their effect. Let them study the table and then, as a check, write the following sentences on the board. Ask which seems to suggest more women doctors. (Answer: 2)

1 Barely a third of all doctors in the USA are women.

2 Almost a third of all doctors in the USA are women.

Key: See Student's Book, page 259.

17 ▶ Avoiding gridlock

To set the ball rolling …

Find out who can drive, who plans to learn, etc., and follow this with a brief topic discussion, e.g. *What are the advantages/disadvantages of owning a car? What are the alternatives?* NB It's best to avoid going into issues covered in the unit in any depth (the benefits of cycling, road safety hazards, safe vs dangerous drivers, traffic problems and solutions).

Lead-in *(p.168)*

This section is useful for revising some key language patterns as well as for raising awareness and it's worth devoting at least 15–20 minutes to it.

- topic vocab including: *traffic jam/congestion, exhaust fumes/car emissions, urban, rush hour*

- useful language for Writing Task 1 including: comparatives, qualifiers like *just/only/over*, and expressions like *constitute, an average of, typically*, etc.

1 Before they do the matching task, ask students to cover the sentence endings **a–h** and try to guess endings for the sentence openings (1–8). Then go through the list, helping them to notice logical or grammatical clues. For example:

1 constitute (= make up): likely to be followed by a percentage or proportion
2 increase; needs adverb (e.g. significantly) or *by* + percentage
3 stuck in traffic: needs *for* + period of time or number of times per week/month/year
4 26 times: needs comparative, e.g. cheaper/more expensive
5 in a car? by bus? by bike? Ask what students think.
6 despite is followed by ? (*-ing* form or noun)
7 wastes: ask what students think (e.g. time? fuel?)
8 cause: ask what students think (pollution? illness?)

2 Let students work in pairs to discuss possible answers before referring to the Key to exercises 1 and 2 on page 254. Give them time to make corrections to their answers so they have an accurate record of these facts.

3 Discuss these questions as a class.

The graphs in the margin offer useful practice in describing and comparing data. You could ask some focus questions to help students 'read' the data first, then let them make sentences describing the information, e.g. *The two countries which make **by far the most** use of bicycles in the EU are Denmark and the Netherlands. In the UK, people cycle **less than half as many** kilometres as the EU average*, etc.

Focus on reading 1 *Avoiding gridlock (p.169)*

It's worth pointing out that this text comes from an American source and contains a number of examples of American spelling and vocabulary. Explain that reading passages in the exam may feature British, Australian or American English, and while there may be slight differences in style, spelling or vocabulary between them, these should not affect understanding. NB *Key Language* Exercise 31 practises British vs American vocabulary (see below).

1 Give students time to answer questions 1–3, and discuss ideas briefly.

2 Locating information tasks are similar to matching heading tasks in that both require you to match information to sections of a text. The difference is that headings *summarise* information in a section whereas these questions *pick out specific information*, and it may be worth checking that students are clear about this. Read through (or elicit) the *Task Approach* first. If necessary, refer students back to the *Task Approach* on page 132. When checking, ask students to justify their answers as usual.

3 Check whether students remember the procedure for sentence completion tasks (What are the two versions? Are the answers in passage order? What's the first step?) and refer them to the *Exam Briefing* and *Task Approach* on page 33 if necessary. When checking, ask them to identify the relevant sections of text.

4 Remind students about the general strategies for tackling a completion task (see *Exam Briefing*, page 91). Let them study the *Task Approach* and flow-chart, and make sure they understand how the information is organised and how the questions are arranged (clockwise or anti-clockwise?). Let them compare answers before checking.

KEY LANGUAGE

- **British vs American vocabulary**
  Exercise 31, page 233
  Suggested approach for classwork
  Ask students to cover the jumbled answers and identify any expressions they know or can guess, before matching the remaining items. This task checks some basic topic vocabulary and could be extended to include other useful items as appropriate.

Focus on vocabulary *More or less? (p.172)*

Point out that synonyms are commonly used to avoid repetition within a text, and that this exercise focuses on alternative ways of expressing an increase or decrease. The important thing is to recognise the broad meaning, rather than the precise connotations of a word. For this reason, it's best not to spend too long differentiating between words during the checking phase.

NB There are detailed notes on words for increasing and decreasing in the Essay Activator section of the *Longman Exams Dictionary*.

Focus on speaking *On four wheels (p.173)*

Remind students that they identified certain facts from *Lead-in* exercise 1 as potentially relevant to topic 1 and ask them to locate these.

It might be helpful to use this topic for a whole-class discussion, as a way of illustrating different ways of balancing the arguments, using expressions from the *Useful language* box.

e.g. **In some ways I agree**, *because without cars people would have to use public transport, and that would be good for the environment. It would cut down on the use of fossil fuels and reduce air pollution.* **Having said that**, *it would make life very difficult for people in country areas or for mothers with small children ….*

It's worth reminding students to pay attention to the grammatical structure and/or tense in the question, and to use this as a guide to answering. e.g. conditional in topic 1; use of modals in topics 3 and 4. It's also worth revising **It depends (on)**, which can be useful in many such topics (see *Useful language*, page 149).

Ask pairs to select one or more topics, depending on the time available, and talk together for 4 to 5 minutes. Monitor their conversations and ask them to summarise the main point afterwards.

KEY LANGUAGE

- **Topic vocabulary: cars and traffic**
  Exercise 32, page 233
  This exercise also provides an opportunity for a useful topic discussion. Ask which of the traffic problems are most serious (and why), which solutions are most effective, what is the reason for increasing cases of road rage, etc.

Focus on reading 2 *Demolishing stereotypes (p.173)*

NB Although shorter than a typical IELTS reading passage, this text provides useful task practice.

1/2 Let students discuss the questions in pairs and then briefly as a class, without confirming or denying any of their ideas. They can find the answer to question 2 in the text.

NB There is an optional Task 1 *Writing Practice* related to this topic (see page 67), which includes practice in interpreting data. This task could be set before or after the reading text, as appropriate.

3 *Questions 5–9*: Although this is the first example of a classification task, it closely resembles Matching tasks, which students have had plenty of practice in. It would be helpful to read through the introduction and *Task Approach* but students will see that the advice is very much as for most other reading tasks.

Questions 10–14: It's worth asking students to spell out the difference between the three possible answers once again. Although this may seem like overkill, this remains one of the trickiest areas of the Reading paper, and students need to be totally confident in tackling it. To reinforce these guidelines, check the answers thoroughly. Make sure students can identify the line number(s) and expressions which provide the evidence.

- **TRUE**: The statement contains the same information as the text, but may express this differently. *Look for synonyms, parallel expressions and summarising statements.*
- **FALSE**: The statement mentions information from the text, but this is inaccurate. *If you make the statement negative, it will be true according to the text.*
- **NOT GIVEN**: The statement contains information which is not in the text at all. *Making the statement negative does not necessarily make it true according to the text.*

If time allows, you could focus on a few interesting expressions from the text, providing further clarification as necessary, e.g. *violations* (5) (e.g. *of human rights*); *anecdotal* (8); *geared to* (13); *little* vs *a little* (34) NB This language point was covered in the last *Error Hit List* on page 166; *nod off* (51); *combat* (56); *addressed* (58).

Optional language focus: cohesive devices.
Remind students what a fundamental feature of
written English cohesive devices are, and how
recognising them is essential to effective reading.

Find the words in the text and say what they refer to.
(line numbers are given in brackets).

1 otherwise (9)   4 It (18)
2 it (12)   5 those (29)
3 this (16)   6 such (31)

Answers
1 (that) women are beginning to drive as
  aggressively than men
2 the question (of whether, as drivers, women differ
  from men)
3 the increase in women drivers
4 age
5 accidents
6 (accidents) which take place in the dark

NB *Key Language* Exercise 10, page 217 has a checklist
of common reference links, which would provide useful
revision.

You could finish this secton by personalising the topic
with a brief discussion. Ask which of the driver types
from page 173 (if any) would be typical in students'
own countries or cultures, and what other road safety
hazards (if any) there might be.

WRITING PRACTICE

- **Presenting and comparing data (guided practice)**
  Exercise 16, page 249

Unit 17 Key

Lead-in *(p.168)*
See Student's Book, page 254.

Focus on reading 1 *(p.169)*
2 1 G 2 B 3 I 4 F 5 D
3 6 E (Section C)
   7 G (*the dispersal of species*, Section D)
   8 F (*changes in urban design*, Section F)
   9 B (Section G)
4 10 global car fleet (Section B)
   11 cars (*cars become essential*, Section C)
   12 (Nearly) a million (Section D)
   13 (a) watershed (Section D)
   14 (air) pollution (Section E)

Focus on vocabulary *(p.172)*
1 A balloon, boost, escalate, rise, sprawl, spread,
     surge, widen
   B diminish, drop, dwindle, fall, lessen, shrink,
     restrict
2 1 rise
   2 restrict
   3 fall
   4 widen
   5 boost
   6 spread
   7 lesson
   8 escalate

Focus on reading 2 *(p.173)*
3 1 (they seek) independence (line 7)
   2 women (drivers) (15)
   3 age (17–19)
   4 55 (31–33)
   5 B (lines 38–40)
   6 A (51–53)
   7 C (47–49)
   8 A (42–43)
   9 B (24–26)
   10 T (lines 8–10)
   11 T (11–14)
   12 F (28–30)
   13 T (45–46)
   14 NG

18 ▶ Small world

To set the ball rolling ...

Discuss one or more of the following quotes and/or build up a mindplan on the subject of Tourism as a way of activating topic vocabulary and exploring various aspects of the subject: social/sociological, economic, ecological, etc.

- *The whole object of foreign travel is not to set foot on foreign land. It is at last to set foot on one's own country as a foreign land.* G.K. Chesterton
- *Vacation: cramming a year's worth of living into a period of approximately two weeks, in an attempt to relax from the rigours of work.* Rick Bayan, *The Cynic's Dictionary.*
- *A perpetual holiday is a good working definition of hell.* George Bernard Shaw

Lead-in *(p.178)*

1 Ask students what the picture shows (tour groups being photographed in front of the Parthenon in Athens, Greece) and then let them discuss the questions in pairs. Afterwards, invite feedback and ask students to mention any relevant personal experience they may have. You could then open up a class discussion on topics such as: *Does travel broaden the mind? Is it better to travel alone or in a tour group? What is the effect of large numbers of tourists visiting ancient monuments? Are cheap air fares a good thing?* etc.

2 After students have checked the answers to questions 1 and 2 on page 255, give them details of the complete top tens (see Key on page 70) and discuss the topic in more depth:
   - *What makes the top three tourist destinations so popular? Are there any surprises in the top ten? Which countries might change position in or enter the top ten soon?*
   - *What do you notice about the top ten tourist spenders?* (e.g. They're all rich, industrialised countries.) NB You could mention that 80% of tourism is made up of nationals from just twenty countries.

Additional speaking practice
To personalise the topic and practise students' critical thinking skills, ask them to suggest a few famous tourist attractions and write 8–10 of these on the board, e.g. *Parthenon, Disneyland, British Museum.* Find out if anybody has visited any of them and, if so, briefly, what they thought of them.

Next, ask them to work in pairs to think of five different ways of categorising the attractions. You could suggest natural vs manmade as an example. Other categories might include: modern vs historical, free to visit vs pay to visit, look at from afar vs enter, interesting vs not interesting for children, etc. Invite pairs to report back and discuss their ideas.

You could also give some practice for Part 1 of the Interview by asking:
- Which tourist attraction in the world would you most like to visit? Why?
- Which would you be least interested in? Why?

These questions provide a good opportunity for using cleft sentences (see *Useful language* page 78 and the teaching notes for that section on page 33.)
The thing I'd most like to see is …
The main reason I want to go there is …
What attracts/interests me most is …

Focus on speaking 1 *Tourism* *(p.179)*

1 Clarify vocabulary as necessary when students have completed the task, then ask them to use the vocabulary to write sentences about places in their own country.

2 Read through the introduction and show how the two sounds /e/ and /eɪ/ when spoken together quickly result in the diphthong /ə/. Introduce the two other diphthongs in turn and practise the sounds in the example countries. Let students compare answers to the task before checking.

3 This activity provides plenty of scope for a discussion of the downside of tourism. When students report back, encourage them to mention any personal experience they have, and to speculate about reasons for tourists' insensitivity.

Ask them to comment on any differences between their answers and the results of the survey on page 255.

NB The negative effects of tourism on local communities in developing countries is a topic in *Focus on writing 1*, page 181.

Focus on listening 1 *Worldwide student projects (p.180)*

Give students time to read through the *Task Advice* and study the questions. To check how effectively they've done this, ask how many task types there are (3) and which questions are likely to be, or include, a number (6, 10).

Focus on writing 1 *Presenting the solution to a problem (p.181)*

Read through the introduction and take the opportunity to check that students remember the difference between the two main approaches, **evidence-led** and **thesis-led**. Depending on your students' needs, you may want to work through one or both of the *Key Language* exercises on conditionals and ways of expressing probability in advance.

Previous discussions should have provided plenty of material for this topic, which is suitable for timed exam practice or homework.

NB There is an example answer for this task type in the *Writing Practice Bank*, page 236. This would be useful to refer to as revision, even if students have already answered the Focus questions.

Focus on speaking 2 *Time off (p.181)*

1/2 Clarify vocabulary as necessary when students have completed the tasks and check that they are using it correctly to talk about the discussion points.

3–5 These tasks cover the three parts of the Speaking test, and students could work through them for the experience of a full interview. In this case, explain the procedure carefully (e.g. one student will be examiner for the three parts before swapping roles) and decide who will provide time checks. Ask students to read through the reminders for each part first. Alternatively, you could deal with each part separately, giving feedback as appropriate.

Focus on listening 2 *The end of oil (p.183)*

Again, ask students to look at the questions, then ask how many task types there are (4 tasks, but only 3 task types).

When there are several task-types and a lot of detail like this, it may not be possible to study every question in advance. Ask students which tasks they think they should concentrate on and establish that they should study the pie chart (noting roughly how it's divided), and try to underline key words in (questions 7–9).

Focus on writing 2 *Dealing with different data (p.184)*

As this is the last task focusing on interpreting and presenting data, it's a good idea to have a round-up of key advice. Students could work in pairs to complete the *Reminders* before checking answers on page 253, or alternatively you could do this as a whole-class activity.

In relation to this specific task, you could also:
* draw their attention to the bar marked EU average and elicit or check expressions like *(well) above/below average*, etc.
* remind them about the need to vary expressions, e.g. *Britain, the British, Britons, British drivers, car use in the UK.*

NB There is a gapped example answer in the *Writing Practice Bank*, although there are many alternative ways of completing the task.

WRITING PRACTICE

* **Task 1: Comparing data (guided practice)**
  Exercise 17, page 250

Unit 18 Key

Lead in (p.178)
2 See Student's Book, page 255.
Additional information
1 (*Total visitors in millions*)
1 **France (79)**
2 **Spain (58)**
3 **United States (51)**
4 China (49)
5 Italy (41)
6 UK (30)
7 Germany (23)
8 Mexico (21)
9 Austria (20)
10 Russia (20)
Figures from The Economist Pocket World in Figures

2 (*$ millions*)
1 **United States (74)**
2 **Germany (73)**
3 **UK (61)**
4 Japan (38)
5 France (32)
6 Italy (22)
7 China (22)
8 Canada (19)
9 Russia (18)
10 Netherlands (16)
Figures from The Economist Pocket World in Figures

Focus on speaking 1 (p.179)
1 1 destinations
2 class
3 office
4 industry
5 resorts
6 attraction
2 1 eight, freight, grey, weigh
2 buy, height, light, while
3 freer, we're, sphere, year
3 See Student's Book, page 255.
4 (*Example answers*)
- Tourist destinations could limit visitor numbers in any one year (as Bhutan does, for example).
- A tourist tax could be imposed to fund spending on conservation or infrastructure.
- There could be legal requirements that international developers protect or improve the local environment.
- International developers could be required to work in partnership with local firms, so that a proportion of the profits remains in the local economy.
- Tour companies should brief representatives and tourists better, particularly with regard to cultural and religious matters.

Focus on listening 1 (p.180)
1 international understanding   **2** improvement
3 Japanese   **4** holiday centre   **5** (very) basic
conditions   **6** 250   **7** disabled   **8** (a) passport
photo   **9** terms and conditions   **10** 1/a/one month

Focus on speaking 2 (p.181)
1 a) job, pay, season
b) agent, expenses, sickness
c) camping, package, skiing
d) air, rail, space
2 (*Example answers*) (taken from the *Longman Exams Dictionary*)
a) Someone who talks or reads about being a traveller, or watches travel programmes on TV, but does not have any real experience of doing it.
b) A place that many tourists visit, but where drinks, hotels, etc. are more expensive – used to show disapproval.
c) The business of organising holidays to natural areas ... such as the rainforest, where people can visit and learn about the area in a way that will not harm the environment.

Focus on listening 2 (p.183)
1 Credit   **2** global warming   **3** 3,000 (three thousand)   **4** transportation   **5** industry
6 buildings   **7** former Soviet Union, Mexico
8 USA, Germany, Japan   **9** South Korea, India
10 B

Focus on writing 2 (p.184)
1 See Student's Book, page 255.
2 (*Suggested answers*)
1 **A**: distance travelled by car; **B**: distance travelled by alternative transport (bus/train/metro/bike); **C**: time spent commuting
2 **A** and **B**: distance (kilometres per year)/selected EU countries (+ EU average); **C**: time (minutes per day)/selected EU countries (+ EU average)
3 Six countries; the average of all the EU countries
4 Denmark has **the highest** car use (approximately 12,500 km per year), while Spain has **the lowest** (around 9,000 km per year). The average Danish person therefore drives about 3,500 km more per year than the average Spanish person.
5 The country which makes **the greatest use** of alternative transport is Denmark. Danish people travel over 3,000 km a year by bus, train, metro or bike, which is **almost double** the EU average (1,800 km) and **over three times** the UK figure (1,000 km).
6 About 48 minutes/**Just under** 50 minutes.
7 Denmark and Italy make **the most use** of alternative transport. Italians spend **the least time** commuting of all the countries represented, about 23 minutes, which is **around half** the EU average. Danes spend **just under** 40 minutes commuting, which is **roughly the same as** the EU average.

Reflective Learning 5 *(p.187)*

Useful vocabulary: prioritise/priority, allot, track (progress), adjust, commitment

Begin with a brief discussion to find out what students understand by 'Time management', how they think it applies to studying for IELTS, and how good they think their own time management is! Avoid confirming or correcting their ideas at this stage.

1/2 Invite brief feedback after the pairwork in each case. It would be useful to find out which of the exam tasks students are not confident of being able to complete in the designated time so that you can build in some practice.

3/4 Talk through the *Ideas for managing study time* and ask which strategies students might be interested in trying. If you can persuade the whole class to keep a study diary, at least for while, this would be both useful for them and a very interesting topic for regular discussion. As a lesser commitment, you could encourage students to allot a specific amount of work time (e.g. 20 minutes a day for a week) to specific areas of study (e.g. revising vocabulary or analysing mistakes in written work). Make a point of checking on students' progress in this area in a few days.

Ask them to report back on their progress towards the learning goal of eliminating a favourite mistake (*Reflective Learning 4*). Emphasise the positive and focus on any success, however small. Offer final advice and encouragement as necessary.

Key: See Student's Book, page 259.

19 ▶ Face value

To set the ball rolling ...

You could begin by mentioning that one of Leonardo da Vinci's favourite techniques for stimulating thinking was to list all the possible distinctions in something. He would begin with basic features and then list variations under each one. So to revise some topic vocabulary, draw a simple face on the board and list the **basic features** *nose, chin, cheek, complexion*, etc. then look at **variations** *round/oval in shape, a pale/dark complexion, unshaven/clean shaven*, etc. and **facial expressions** *smile, blush, frown*, etc. *look happy/sad/angry/surprised*, etc.

You could also add one or two **idioms**, but stick to ones which are appropriate to IELTS topics, e.g. *a face-to-face discussion, lose/save face*. These last two are well worth discussing, especially in a multi-cultural class. They may also be relevant to the second part of the *Lead-in*.

Lead-in *(p.188)*

1 Introduce the topic and clarify vocabulary if necessary, e.g. *contempt* and *disgust*. Let students check answers and discuss how 'universally' recognisable these expressions are.

2 Let students work through the questions in pairs and then open a whole-class discussion. Questions 2 and 3 are potentially very productive topics, particularly in terms of interesting cultural differences.

  2 You could get a few students to each demonstrate a gesture and see if the class can say what they mean. Find out what gestures from other cultures they know of. Discuss how gestures can add to or change a verbal message, or replace it altogether.

  3 Find out if anyone has relevant personal experience to describe. If students are short of ideas, give a few prompts and then let them fill in the details, e.g. *a meal where you are the honoured guest, an encounter with a wild animal, a consumer complaint.*

Focus on speaking 1 *Face the facts 1 (p.189)*

Students will be able to compare their answers to these questions with information in the reading section to follow, so keep feedback to a minimum.

Focus on reading 1 *Face the facts 2 (p.189)*

1/2 Set a tight time limit to encourage the use of skimming/scanning skills, before checking answers to questions 1 and 2 in exercise 1. Let students read the extracts in more detail before discussing answers to exercise 2.

3 This language area has been practised in earlier units and, if students haven't done so already, they could complete the tasks in *Key Language* Exercise 10 (page 217) as revision.

4 Make sure students are really studying the words in context, and ask them to compare ideas before checking. NB It's worth eliciting the noun from *collide (collision)*, since this is tested in *Focus on vocabulary*.

Focus on reading 2 *Face (p.190)*

This is the last exam reading passage, so little additional support should be needed. However, you may want to review general strategies one last time:
- **Always read the instructions carefully**. There may be slight variations from task to task.
- **Skim the passage to form a general picture first**. Don't waste time on detailed reading until you find out what information is important.
- **Glance through the questions and underline key words**. This will tell you what parts of the text to focus on and what information you need to look for.
- **Identify the relevant sections of the text that you need to read in detail**. This is based on the topics covered in the questions,

Allow students as near to the target exam time of 20 minutes as possible and be prepared to analyse answers in some depth afterwards.

Focus on vocabulary *Word building (p.193)*

If time is short, these tasks are suitable for self-study, since exercise 1 can be checked using a dictionary, and answers to exercise 3 can be found in the texts, using the references in brackets.

Focus on speaking 2 *Dress the part (p.194)*

These tasks allow students to role-play Part 2 and Part 3 of the Interview. The two parts can be tackled separately, with both students discussing a Part 1 topic before moving on to Part 2. However, if the procedures are thoroughly familiar, and the Speaking test is looming, you might prefer each student to work through two parts before swapping roles.

1/2 Give students time to read through the *Reminders* and check that they are clear about the instructions. Divide them into pairs, allot initial roles and make sure they have some means of checking time. Once the interviews are under way, monitor to ensure that students are following the correct procedure, and note down points for feedback.

3 Read through the instructions and *Reminders*, and make sure students are aware of the timing for this part of the interview (4 to 5 minutes). It's important to include feedback on these discussions, so if time is limited, you could specify (or let students select) just two or three topics.

Unit 19 Key

Lead-in *(p.188)*
1 See Student's Book, page 255.

Focus on reading 1 *(p.189)*
1 1 C 2 A 3 D 4 B
3 1 misunderstandings caused by the absence of body language and/or facial expression
  2 see the expression
  3 the facial movements previously mentioned (averted gaze, brief smile, etc.)
  4 defendants
  5 the child
  6 face-to-face communication (with parents and peers)
4 (*Example answers*)
  1 bump into each other
  2 likely (to)
  3 concise/using few words
  4 not sorry
  5 broken (of rules, laws)
  6 vitally/extremely important
  7 children of their own age
  8 response

Focus on reading 2 *(p.190)*
1 (It's) more mobile (para. B)
2 *frontalis, risorius* (in any order) (C)
3 at birth (C)
4 (the) nose (D)
5 lie detection (E)
6 Descend (C)
7 Rise and arch (D)
8 Retract(ed) horizontally (C)
9 Tighten (D)
10 straight down (H)
11–13 C, D, F (in any order) (H)
14 B (G)
15 C (I)
16 D (J)

Focus on vocabulary *(p.193)*
1 1 appearance
  2 apparent
  3 collision
  4 communication
  5 communicative
  6 deception
  7 deceptive
  8 emphasise/ize
  9 emphatic
  10 enjoyment
  11 enjoyable
  12 existence
  13 existent, existing
  14 identification
  15 identifiable
  16 intention
  17 intentional, intended
  18 respond
  19 responsive
  20 widen
  21 width
2 1 deceptive
  2 existence
  3 response
  4 emphatic
  5 collision
  6 widen
  7 apparent
  8 communication
  9 intentional
  10 identify
3 1 into
  2 on
  3 In
  4 to
  5 in
  6 at
  7 in, for
  8 in
  9 on
  10 On at
  11 of
  12 to

20 ▶ Through the lens

To set the ball rolling ...

Ask students to complete the sentence *A picture is worth a thousand ...?* (Answer: *words*) and discuss this common saying briefly, e.g. *Think of a situation when this is particularly true. Why are pictures so powerful? Do you prefer instructions to be in words or pictures?*

Lead-in (p.198)

1 When students have had a few moments' discussion in pairs, invite general feedback and ask for comments on the special qualities of each medium. Use this opportunity to find out if anyone is particularly interested in one of the media.

  2 Make it clear that they should identify the general uses or categories of photography illustrated, e.g. formal portraits, rather than specific subject matter. Ask pairs to list uses and then team up with another pair and compare lists.

  In feedback, ask students to suggest other related uses of photography, e.g. *formal portraits*: passport/identity card photos; *medical*: micro cameras which can travel through the body. You could also broaden the discussion to include other uses of photography including *aerial* (for mapmaking, weather forecasting, etc.), *education/training* (visual aids), etc.

2 Use the examples to remind students about *syllables* and *stress* and give brief practice. When checking, clarify the meaning of any unknown items, especially those relating to photography, e.g. *enlargement, negative, perspective, projector.*

Focus on listening 1 *Photography courses (p.199)*

You may prefer students to tackle the two listening sections consecutively without the interruption of the Film Quiz. In this case, let students discuss the quiz before the listening practice.

Begin these last two listening practices with a round-up of key advice, e.g.
* Check how many **task-types** there are and read the **instructions** for each set.
* Study the headings and lay-out of **tables** carefully.
* Read through the questions as far as you can and think about **possible answers**.
* When you have to choose words from **a list**, think about the **pronunciation** in advance.

Focus on listening 2 *History of cinema (p.200)*

> **Additional notes on Film Quiz**
> *Question 1*: note that although modern photography began in France in the 19th century, the development of the camera goes back much further, as students will hear when they listen to the recording.
> *Question 5*: The Indian film industry is the largest in terms of ticket sales and number of films produced each year, while the American film industry is the largest in terms of revenue.

Focus on speaking *Practice interview (p.202)*

If you want to deal with each part separately, revise key advice beforehand, let each student practise their topic, and give feedback before moving on to the next part.

Alternatively, students can work through all three parts before swapping roles and repeating the procedure. In this case, have a round-up of key advice for all three parts first, and make sure students know exactly what to do before they begin.

Part 1
* **Listen carefully** and make sure you answer the questions which are put (not a similar question you've prepared for!).
* Give **full answers** with reasons or examples, whenever possible.

Part 2
* Make **brief notes**, perhaps using a mindplan, to ensure you cover all the points on the topic card.
* This is your opportunity to demonstrate your fluency. Try to use a **good range of vocabulary** and **structure**, and to keep talking for at least a minute.

Part 3
* Don't be afraid to ask for **clarification**, e.g. *I'm not sure if I understand the question. Could you explain?*
* Give **reasons** and/or **examples** to illustrate your point of view.
* Remember to **link your ideas** (e.g. *not only ... but also ...; On the other hand, ...*).

NB There is a *Writing Practice* task based on one of the discussion topics in this section, which is suitable for class or homework (see page 75).

WRITING PRACTICE

- **Task 2: Presenting and justifying an opinion (exam task)**
  Exercise 18, page 250

Focus on writing *Describing an object (p.203)*

1/2 Let students read through the *Exam Briefing* and then give them a few moments to look through the task on page 205. They may well find this a bit daunting and to reassure them, ask them to estimate how many words will be needed to describe each camera from the total of around 150. In fact, allowing for the introductory sentence, only a basic description of each is possible.

Ask them to study the *Task Approach* notes, and then discuss question 2.

3 Check and practise these expressions as necessary. It would be useful to focus on each pattern in turn and ask students to use the expressions to describe some everyday items, e.g. *a ruler, a plate, a chess board, a swimming pool, a football pitch*, etc. For further practice, you could make incorrect statements about the objects in exercise 4 and invite students to correct them, e.g. *The longcase clock has a height of 3m.*

4 Students could either work on this task in pairs (if they're reasonably able) or, for more support, you could treat this as a whole-class activity. In either case, it would be useful for them to make a written record of some of this key language in context.

5 Let students study the instructions and diagrams in detail and refer back the *Task Approach* if necessary. Elicit a few descriptions orally, encouraging them to make use of the expressions listed and to use alternatives for *was invented*.

Give them 20 minutes to complete the task. The gapped model answer and/or the additional writing topic (see below) can then be set for homework.

NB There is a gapped model answer for this question in the *Writing Practice Bank*, but students will benefit most if they attempt their own answers first. For further practice there is also an exam task on describing objects.

WRITING PRACTICE

- **Task 1: Describing objects (guided practice)**
  Exercise 19, page 251
- **Task 1: Describing objects (exam task)**
  Exercise 20, page 252

Unit 20 Key

Lead-in (p.198)

1 2 A advertising (property)
  B portrait
  C amateur photography (holiday snaps)
  D news/sport reportage (horse race)
  E medical (X-ray)
  F crime prevention/detection (CCTV image)

3 A accessory, advertisement, photographer, technology, transparency
  B advertise, cinema, digital, negative, photograph
  C commercial, develop, enlargement, perspective, projector
  D landscape, portrait, programme, tripod, wildlife

Focus on listening 1 (p.199)

1 Foundation
2 Intermediate
3 2–4.30
4 16 weeks
5 (at) any time/flexitime
6 60 hours
7 B, E (in any order)
8 A
9 B
10 B

Focus on listening 2 (p.200)

1 See Student's Book, page 255.
See additional notes on page 74.

2 1 drawing
2 entertainment
3 one person
4 projection system
5 Train Robbery
6 full-length sound
7 (Disney) cartoon
8–10 (in any order) cheap land (available), low wages, (incredibly) varied landscapes

Focus on writing (p.203)

2 (*Example answers*)
was introduced, appeared, became available

4 (*Example answers*)
A The wristwatch **consists of** a small clock and a strap (which is) **made of** leather. The clock section is **circular** and **made of** stainless steel. It has a black face with **a diameter of** 3cm.
B The alarm clock is rectangular **in shape**. It is 10cm **high by** 8cm **wide,** and **made of** plastic.
C The longcase clock **consists of** a wooden case which **contains** a clock. It **has a height of** 2m. The clock has a brass face **with a diameter of** 36cm.
D Big Ben **has an overall height of** 96.3m. It **consists of** two parts, a lower section **measuring** 76m, which is **made of** brick, and a smaller upper section **measuring** 20.3m **containing** the clock, which **is made** of cast iron. The clock face **has a diameter of** 7m.
• Big Ben is approximately **50 times taller** than the longcase clock. / The height of Big Ben is approximately **50 times greater** than that of …
• The wristwatch is only **a fraction of the size of** the longcase clock.
• The alarm clock is **more complex** than the wristwatch.
• The longcase clock is **considerably heavier than** the alarm clock.

Critical Thinking 5 (p.207)

Begin by revising the term *argument* (an opinion supported by reasons, see page 87) and remind students of the importance of providing sufficient evidence to support an argument.

When you've read through the main introduction, it's worth taking a few moments to discuss the issue of **plagiarism**. This can be defined as: "*copying or closely imitating someone else's ideas and representing them as if they were your own*". Point out that plagiarism is a form of theft, which is taken very seriously in the academic world. Explain that if a student's work is found to contain plagiarism, they will certainly lose marks, and in serious cases, their work may be rejected completely, which could affect their academic career.

It's important to be aware of what is considered plagiarism. Ask which of the following would be acceptable in an academic context? (Answer: d)
a) submitting an essay that you've bought online
b) copying an essay from another student
c) mentioning information from the internet without acknowledgement
d) mentioning something that is common knowledge without giving an original source

Look at the introductions to the two sections on *Reporting language* and *Indicating attitude* together and then let students work through the exercises, either individually or in pairs. When checking, discuss possible answers in detail.

Key: See Student's Book, page 259.

▶ Recording script

Unit 2, Focus on listening 1
Students' Union survey (p.22)

I = Interviewer; S = Student

I Hi, I'm from the Students' Union. **We're doing a survey of students' eating habits.** Is it all right if I ask you a few questions?

S Will it take long?

I No, not really. Five minutes maybe? There aren't all that many questions.

S And what's it for exactly?

I Well, we wanted to get an idea of the sort of things students eat on a regular basis, and find out how aware people are about diet and nutrition and things. **The idea is to produce an information leaflet about healthy eating.**

S Yeah, I suppose something like that'd be quite useful, a leaflet I mean, especially for new students. Anyway, what do you want to know, exactly?

I OK, first question. What would you say your favourite food is?

S That's easy. **A burger and chips. Lots of chips!** I must say I like a nice Chinese meal as well, and maybe spaghetti once in a while … But no, the best has got to be a burger.

I OK, and what's your least favourite food?

S Hm. Let me think. I've never been that keen on cauliflower. Or fish – the smell puts me off. But no, **the thing I really can't stand is salad.** Rabbit food, I call it. I know lettuce and things are supposed to be healthy and all that, but it's just not a real meal, is it?

I Mm. Tut tut. You're getting into some bad habits there, you know. Anyway, moving on … Let's take a typical day. How many meals do you have? I mean proper sit-down meals, not snacks.

S Well, I nearly always oversleep, which means I generally skip breakfast altogether. And then I'd probably just have a bar of chocolate for lunch. So in answer to your question, **I don't sit down to a proper meal till the evening.**

I OK. Typical student, I suppose! And the next question: How many eggs would you eat in a week? One? Two?

S Well, I don't do much cooking as a rule, but **every Sunday I make myself a nice fried breakfast as a treat. That's sausages, bacon and two eggs**, the works. Lovely!

I That sounds OK once a week. But I wouldn't recommend it on a regular basis. Too much fat. And how about fresh fruit? Does it figure in your diet at all?

S Naah, not really, well, I know it's bad, but … I'm just not in the habit really. I suppose **I might eat an apple once in a blue moon**. But that's about it.

I Pity. But I suppose it's better than nothing! And would you say you had a sweet tooth?

S I guess so. Well, most people have, haven't they? Me, I can't resist a bar of chocolate.

I OK, one more question: is eating healthily important to you at all? I mean, would you choose one thing rather than another because it was more healthy?

S No, I can't say that I would. I don't really think there's any difference in taste. **I think all this craze for organic food is rubbish. It's just a way to make money.**

I OK. Well, that's more or less it, apart from the last section.

I If I could just take a couple of personal details? Your name? It's not obligatory, actually …

S That's all right. I'm Jamie **Buckingham**.

I Is that Buckingham as in the palace?

S Sorry? Yeah, that's right. **B-U-C-K-I-N-G-H-A-M**.

I Mm-hm. Got that. And which course are you on, Jamie?

S **I'm doing a degree in Travel and Tourism.**

I Mm! Lucky you! That's in the Business Studies Faculty, right?

S Correct.

I And which year are you in?

S I'm in my second year. One more to go!

I Right, that's everything. Thanks a lot for your help.

S No problem. Cheers.

Unit 2, Focus on listening 2
Healthy eating (p.23)

T = Tutor; L = Linda Golding

T I think that's all I need to say at this stage by way of an introduction to the college. But just to round off the morning, we can turn to something different – a subject which I think is close to most people's hearts – food! So let me introduce Linda Golding, the college Welfare Officer – Linda …

L Thank you. Hello, everyone. Yes, I'm here to say a few words about healthy eating. And **the first thing I want to emphasise is the importance of a balanced diet.** The right balance is vitally important for health, both mental and physical, especially when you're studying hard or under stress. I know it's tempting to eat a lot of snacks and take-outs, but remember that they tend to contain a lot of sugar and fat. And we eat too much sugar. Did you know that in Europe and the USA, **we're eating about twenty times as much sugar as we did in 1800**? Shocking, isn't it? And also five times as much fat. No wonder there's been a huge increase in heart disease and other illnesses in the West. So in the short time I've been allotted, I'd like to run through some basic principles.

Now, one of the most important things to include in our diet is fresh fruit and vegetables. The advice is that **we should be aiming to eat five servings every day**. It sounds a lot, I know, but you soon reach that if you have a banana with your breakfast, an apple at lunch and three vegetables with your evening meal.

Secondly, most of us need to try and reduce our sugar intake. Remember that many processed foods and ready meals contain sugar. And the **one thing to be especially careful about is carbonated drinks like lemonade and cola.** They're usually packed full of sugar. So avoid carbonated drinks and choose water or fruit juice instead – it's better for you!

Another thing to watch is your fat intake. Most of the fat in our diet comes from meat and dairy products, so try and stick to lean meat, poultry and fish, and **make a point of choosing low-fat dairy products**, things like yoghurt or skimmed milk. Oh, and don't buy hard cooking fat – use sunflower oil instead.

Next, we all know that cholesterol is a bad word. It's found in meat and dairy products, of course, but don't forget that it's also in eggs. So **limit the number of eggs you eat to three or four a week**. That's what the health experts suggest.

Just a couple more points. Most of us eat far too much salt, and that can lead to high blood pressure. So **cut down the amount of salt you add to food**. When you're cooking, **try using lemon juice instead** as a way of enhancing the flavour.

Finally, don't be tempted to skip meals. It's much better for your health if you **eat regular light meals, three times a day**, rather than just one enormous meal.

Now, just for fun, here's a question for you. What do you think is **the world's most nutritious fruit**? An apple, would you say? Or an orange? Well, you may be surprised – it's actually **an avocado pear.** You know, those dark-green fruits you see in salads sometimes. Avocado pears contain about 165 calories for every 100 grams. That's more than eggs or milk.

They also contain twice as much protein as milk and more Vitamin A, B and C.

Well, that's all I have time for now. And, yes, it's lunchtime, so enjoy your meal and be healthy!

Unit 4, Focus on listening 1
Wasting energy (p.42)

T = Tutor; S = Susan; P = Peter

T Good morning, everyone. Now, whose turn is it to do their mini-presentation today? Peter and Susan? OK, what topic did the two of you decide on in the end?

S We thought we'd have a look at the problem of waste in cities.

T Fine, well, when you're ready.

S OK. One of the many problems about cities is that they create such an enormous amount of rubbish. I've got some figures here to show you … Umm, how does this thing work?

P Press the 'On' button.

S Right … well, as you can see from the graph, New York produces about fifteen million kilograms of waste a day. It's a world record …

P But not exactly one to be proud of!

S No, and **Tokyo comes next with about eleven million**. Basically, the richer the city, the more rubbish it generates. The thing is that in developing countries, much more waste is recycled, so there's less to dispose of. If you compare Los Angeles and Calcutta, for example, they both have roughly the same population, but Los Angeles produces about ten million kilograms of rubbish, while **Calcutta, a much poorer city, only produces half of that, five million kilograms**.

P You forgot to mention Mexico City.

S Yes, Mexico City's huge, but it only generates about seven million kilograms – less than half the figure for New York. Now, the big question is, what do we do with all this rubbish? At the moment, most of it ends up on rubbish tips or buried underground, which is a terrible waste of resources.

S And there's another problem, which Peter will talk about. Over to you, Peter …

P Thanks, Sue. Yes, the other thing is that it can take an incredibly long time for rubbish to biodegrade, that is, to break down and decay. Just to give you an idea, food and other organic material is the quickest to biodegrade. **A loaf of bread decays in about twenty days**, for example, as long as the conditions are right. We throw away tons of newspapers and packaging, and paper takes anything from three months to a year to biodegrade. But **the conditions have to be damp.**

In dry conditions, it can last for decades. Metals take even longer, obviously. Most, like tin or iron, can take anything between one and ten years …

S But that doesn't apply to aluminium, does it? And **80% of soft-drink cans are made of aluminium**.

P No, that's right. Aluminium's a special problem because it doesn't rust. So recycling is really the only answer. And **another major problem is plastics**. There are 80 different types, for a start. Scientists think a typical item like a bottle could take a hundred years to decay. But as plastic has only been around for about a century, we can only really guess. And the longest lasting of all is glass. We know from archaeological evidence that **glass can survive for at least 4,000 years**, and who knows, maybe longer?

S Thanks, Peter. Now, just to round off, I wanted to say a word about some of the factors which can affect the process of biodegrading. One is **temperature** – things decay more quickly when it's warm and more slowly in cool temperatures. Another factor is **humidity**. A moist environment speeds up decay. And the third is **oxygen** – that's a bit more difficult, because some materials, like oil, need the presence of oxygen to break down, while others don't.

T OK. Good work, both of you. Now, are there any questions?

Unit 4, Focus on listening 2
Case study: São Paulo (p.45)

Is everyone here? Good, well, last week we talked about the astonishing growth of the world's cities, if you remember, and today I want to look at some of the reasons for this. What is it that draws people to leave their homes and families and move to big cities? To answer this question, I'm going to take São Paulo in Brazil as an example.

First, some basics. There's a fact sheet on São Paulo in your books, but I think it's slightly out of date, so let me give you the correct information and you can make any changes. OK? Well, **the city dates back to the 16th century – 1554, to be precise**. By 1970, it had a population of 7.8 million; not quite a megacity, but growing fast. I think your book gives the present population as 15.2 million, doesn't it? But **the most recent figure I have is 16.5 million**, which means the population has more than doubled since 1970. That makes São Paulo the world's third largest city, according to UN statistics. But other cities are growing even faster, and if UN projections are correct, by the year 2015, São Paulo will have fallen to the fourth largest city, after Tokyo, Mumbai (formerly Bombay) and Lagos in Nigeria.

São Paulo is South America's leading industrial city, and **two of its most significant manufacturing products are cars and computers**. On the agricultural side, Brazilian coffee is world famous, as you know, and **São Paulo is the country's main centre for the coffee trade**. Now, I hope you managed to get all that …

Now let's look at a survey which was carried out among migrants to São Paulo. These are people living in the 'favelas', or shanty towns, on the outskirts of the city, and the aim was to find out why they'd decided to leave their homes and move there.

One set of reasons for migration are described as 'push factors'. A typical push factor was that there had been a poor harvest, for example. Another was that **there wasn't enough money to make improvements to farms**, so old farms remained inefficient and uneconomic to run. Some migrants said that opportunities for education were very limited in the countryside. And others mentioned problems to do with the weather. The main reason given here was **floods**. **Floods** occur from time to time after heavy rain, and they **can cause terrible damage to farmland, homes and other property**.

Another set of reasons are 'pull factors', or factors which attracted migrants into the city. The main pull factor people mentioned was that **cities offered more variety of work**. Employment opportunities are obviously much more limited in the countryside. In addition, migrants mentioned that wages are much higher in São Paulo than they are for similar work in smaller towns and villages. Another pull factor mentioned in the survey was **entertainment opportunities**, things like cinemas, clubs and sporting events. And we all know how the Brazilians love football! People also mentioned the fact that there were **better hospitals and health facilities available in town**. Last but not least, some people said that if your relations already live in the city, it makes the move easier, because you have someone to help you settle in, find work, etc.

The survey also looked at 'migration obstacles', that is things which can stop migrants moving to the city. The main one here is a question of money. Unless you can walk to the city or hitch a lift, **you need to pay for transport. If you're poor, this can be a major stumbling block**. Secondly, members of your family may object to the idea of your moving away. And that, too, can be a difficult obstacle to overcome.

Well, that's all I have to say on the São Paulo case study, but if you're interested in following it up or finding out more about the city, there's a Reading List on this handout, which I'm going to pass round now …

Unit 6, Focus on listening 1
Student interviews (p.61)

R = Rob; L = Linda Richmond

R Hi, come in. Take a seat. We haven't met before, have we?

L No.

R I didn't think so. Well, I'm Rob, I'm one of the Student Counsellors here. And you are … ?

L Linda Richmond.

R Right. And which course are you on, Linda?

L **I'm doing Computer Studies**.

R OK. Now, the reason for this little chat is that we wanted to find out a bit about what students do when they're not studying. How you relax. What activities you do. Things like that. But in particular, we'd like to know if there's anything we can do to improve the facilities available to students. OK?

L OK.

R So, tell me, where are you living at the moment?

L **On campus**.

R That's good. At least you don't have to worry about commuting if you're on campus.

L No, but it can be a bit of a problem getting into town in the evening.

R I suppose that's true. Swings and roundabouts. But, tell me, do you belong to any of the student clubs?

L Yes, **I joined the Film Society when I first arrived**, and I probably go along two, three times a week. Movies are great – they take your mind off your work and everything.

R Good. And that's it?

L That's it.

R So what do you think of the facilities in general?

L They're quite good. In my opinion, anyway.

R Any suggestions for improvements?

L Well, **I think the one thing that's really needed is a new gym**.

R You don't think the current gym is adequate?

L The thing is, it's nowhere near big enough. You can hardly ever get to use it, except at eight o'clock in the morning maybe. And the equipment's out of the Ark. It really needs updating. No, a new gym would be fantastic.

R OK, and finally are there any other activities you do in your spare time?

L Mm. **I do quite a bit of cooking**. It's the best way I know of relaxing. My speciality is curry! I'm always playing around with new recipes.

R Great. That's been very helpful. Many thanks.

R = Rob; J = Jim Maybury

R OK, so could I have your name?

J **Jim. Jim Maybury.**

R Jim – er, sorry, how do you spell your surname?

J **M-A-Y-B-U-R-Y.**

R Maybury, thanks. And what course are you doing, Jim?

J Marine Biology.

R And how's it going?

J Fine, so far.

R Good, good, and where are you living?

J I've got a place five kilometres from college.

R Excellent. And student clubs, societies … Do you belong to anything in particular?

J Yes, **I'm a member of the Athletics Club**. We've just got back from an inter-university athletics tournament, actually.

R And how did you get on?

J We came second.

R Well done. That's quite an achievement. So you're obviously into sport. And what do you think of the university facilities?

J To be honest, **I think they're a bit limited**. Compared with other universities I know, anyway.

R I see, and what improvements would you like to see?

J **The number one priority, as far as I'm concerned, is a swimming pool.** I can't believe a university this size hasn't got one. It's crazy for students to have to go to the public pool in town.

R Yes, I must say you're not the first person to mention that. Actually, there is talk of a major fund-raising campaign for new facilities, so maybe there's hope on the horizon. Anyway, last question: Do you take part in any other activities? To relax or whatever?

J **I play the guitar mostly**. It's something I've always done and it's great for winding down.

R Terrific. Thanks, Jim. Good luck with the course.

Unit 6, Focus on listening 2
Ten ways to slow down your life (p.62)

We hear an awful lot about stress these days. There seems to be more pressure in everyone's life. So, is there anything we can do about it? Well, I think there is, and I'm going to suggest a few ways of slowing down the pace of life and making things a little less frenetic.

Let's talk about working hours first. Do you find yourself working later each day just to deal with your workload? The problem is that you'll be even less able to cope the next day if you don't give yourself time to relax. So, **my first tip is to set a finishing time, and then make sure you keep to it**. That's unless you have a real crisis to deal with, of course.

Next, what do you do at midday? Do you just eat a sandwich at your desk? Or, worse still, skip lunch altogether? Well, nobody can work efficiently for eight hours non-stop. So the next tip is to **give yourself a proper lunch break, I mean one that lasts at least 30 minutes**, and do try to get away from your desk, get some fresh air.

And what about all those messages which are waiting for a reply? Don't panic. **Start each day by putting things in order of priority. Deal with the most urgent emails, faxes or phone calls first.** The less important ones can wait. Remember, it's important to take control of technology rather than letting technology take control of you.

Now, do you suffer from clutter? I mean all the stuff that lies around on your desk because you don't know what to do with it. **Well, there's a very useful piece of equipment called the wastepaper bin.** And that's the best place for an awful lot of clutter. So use the bin for what it's there for. Be ruthless. You'll tackle the important things much more effectively with a clear desk.

It's important to be realistic. **You won't always be able to clear your in-tray by the time you leave.** But don't worry if there's still some work. The chances are that you'll be able to deal with the in-tray much more efficiently next day.

Remember: work should be fun. Really! But if you do find that things are getting on top of you, go and find someone to talk to. Only, don't talk shop. **Pick something to talk about that's outside work**, a football match, say, or a film. You'll feel much better, believe me.

OK, let's think about home now. The important thing when you get home is to forget about work. Don't go on about the awful day you've had. **Make a point of listening to other people** instead. Find out what's been happening in *their* lives.

And what do you do to relax in the evening? **The main activity for most of us, I'm afraid, is watching television.** The problem with this is that it's a passive activity. It won't recharge your batteries, and it won't re-energise you. **So give the TV a miss** and do something with your friends or family instead. That's far better relaxation.

Another good way to use your leisure time is to do something for someone else. After all, life is about more than making money or passing exams. **Why not get involved in your local community** in some way? You could lend a hand at your local school or old people's home, for example, or help raise money for a local charity.

And finally, why not take up a new activity? Maybe something you've always wanted to do, but weren't sure you were capable of. You could join a painting class, for example, or **take lessons on a musical instrument**. You could even take up a new sport like waterskiing. Why not? You might discover a talent you never knew you had!

And on that positive note, I think I'd better stop, and maybe if there are some questions …

Unit 8, Focus on listening 1
Music festival (p.79)

A = Andy; M = Maria

A Oh, good, Maria, I was hoping to catch you.

M Hi, Andy, what's up?

A Well, there's a group of us thinking of going to the music festival, and we wondered if you'd be interested in coming along.

M Sorry, what music festival?

A Didn't you know? There's going to be a big international music festival here with loads of famous names performing.

M I'm not really into classical music.

A Oh, it's not just classical music. There's all sorts. Just a minute, I've got the programme here. Yes, there's world music from an incredible variety of countries: Scottish and Irish **folk music**, for example, West African percussion, Russian choral music, which should be fantastic, Indian classical music – I could go on and on. And then if you're a **jazz fan**, there's **a special jazz weekend** and also a whole day of contemporary music.

M Any rock music?

A 'Fraid not.

M Still, it sounds interesting. When is it exactly?

A It's in May.

M Oh, I'm going to be away the first week of May. I don't get back till the 12th.

A Well, that's OK because **it doesn't start until the 9th** and we were thinking of going the following weekend, that's Saturday the 16th …

M Fine.

A Anyway, **it's on for a whole fortnight** so there'll be plenty of time to enjoy it.

A Look, let me tell you the things we were thinking of going to and you can say if you're interested in joining us.

M OK.

A Right, well, on the Saturday there's a talk about Cuban music – it's not only a talk, actually, there's a demonstration of all the different styles as well. **That's at half past ten in the morning** and tickets cost £6.

M Sounds great.

A And then in the afternoon, there's something called 'The sounds of Scotland' at two o'clock.

M I love Scottish music.

A Me too. **The tickets for that are £8.** And then, the next day …

M The Sunday?

A Yes. There's a fantastic band from The Gambia, who play all kinds of traditional music, and they've got a stunning lead singer, apparently. The concert's at seven o'clock in the evening and it's called **'Africa Alive'.**

M 'Africa Alive'.

A Yes, the tickets are £15 – they're a bit more expensive, because it's an evening concert, I suppose. What do you think?

M Yes, count me in, definitely.

A Great. Then, getting away from music, they're doing a special **cruise on a canal boat, including lunch** and also a talk about the canal and its history. It's on Sunday afternoon, and **it costs, let me see …. yes, £14.50**.

M I think that might be stretching the budget a bit too far!

A OK, well three out of four isn't bad! And then there are loads of other things going on at the same time as well. Art exhibitions and stuff. We liked the sound of **the Bus Stop Gallery**.

M The what?

A **The Bus Stop Gallery.** It's an art exhibition on a bus which tours around the country. Anyway, the bus is going to be at the festival, and we thought we'd go along some time.

M Why not? Look, shall I give you some money now?

A No, wait till I've got the tickets. By the way, students can get a discount on the price of the tickets, but **you might have to show your student card when you go in, so can you remember to have it with you**?

M Sure.

A Anyway, I must fly. See you.

M Thanks, Andy. Bye

Unit 8, Focus on listening 2 *The Museum of Anthropology (p.80)*

S = Sue; T = Tom Brisley

S It's time for our regular 'Museum of the Week' spot on the programme, and here's Tom Brisley to tell us about it. Where is it you've been, Tom?

T Well, I've just come back from Vancouver, Sue, and I must say I had a fantastic time. There's so much to see and do in the city. But if you get a chance to go there, there's one place you mustn't miss, and that's the Museum of Anthropology. It was certainly one of the highlights of my time in Canada.

The museum was actually established way back in 1949 and these days it's one of the most popular in Canada. It's worth going there just to see the building, in fact, because it's stunningly modern and dramatic – it's hard to believe it was built back in 1976. One very good thing is that **the museum's all on one floor**, which makes it easily accessible for wheelchairs. Another plus is that it's in the most beautiful setting, overlooking the sea. And inside, you can see archaeological and ethnographical material from all over the world, although what **the museum is best known for is its collection of art and culture from the native people of the Pacific North-West**.

It's not a large museum, so it's quite easy to find your way around. When you arrive, you come into an entrance lobby with **a small shop on the right,** where you can buy guidebooks and some interesting souvenirs. Then, if you walk straight ahead, you'll go down a sloping ramp until you come to a kind of crossroads with **an information desk**. It's worth spending a few minutes there, 'cos the staff are very helpful and you can pick up various useful maps and leaflets. If you turn left at this point, there's a large ceramics gallery, and if you turn right, you'll eventually come to the theatre. But instead, keep walking straight ahead in the same direction as the ramp and you'll find yourself in the museum's most impressive room, **the Great Hall**. This was designed to house 30 of the museum's largest totem poles and it's absolutely spectacular! The glass walls are fifteen metres high, and the whole design is based on the structure of the native wooden houses.

After that, you can enjoy just wandering around the various galleries. Don't miss the Rotunda, which is the setting for a beautiful modern sculpture called 'The Raven and the First Men'. It's carved from a huge block of cedar wood and **it took five people over three years to complete**. One of the best things about the museum, by the way, is that nothing is hidden away in store rooms. Everything is on show in a fascinating section called 'Visible storage'.

Now, a few practicalities. The museum is situated on the University of British Columbia campus, which is quite a long way out of Vancouver City, so **you'll** need to take a bus to get there. Take a number 10 or a number 4 from town and stay on till the end of the line.

Finally, it's a good idea to check the opening times before you go. **If you visit in the winter, remember that the museum is closed on Mondays.** During the summer months, it's open daily. It's also worth noting that **there's late opening till nine in the evening on Tuesdays, and that's all year round.** If you want more information, the museum has a useful website, which you'll find on our Factsheet.

S Many thanks for that, Tom. And that report brings us to the end of the programme. And in next week's …

Unit 10, Focus on listening 1
Predicting a volcanic eruption (p.100)

S = Sarah; A = Alan

S Hi, Alan. Long time no see.

A Oh, hi, Sarah.

S You look busy. What is it? An assignment?

A Yes, on volcanoes. But I'm having a bit of trouble with it.

S We did that one last year. What's the problem?

A Well, I'm looking at ways of predicting when a volcano's likely to erupt, and I've come across this diagram …

S Looks interesting. Can I see?

A Sure. It's from a leaflet they give to local people in the Philippines and it shows the different signs to look out for. The trouble is, they're not all labelled.

S Mm. Oh, we can probably work out what the rest are. Let's have a go.

A Oh, OK, great. Well, starting at the top, there's that cloud of smoke or vapour or whatever, and it's at three different levels: high, medium and low. I assume that must be **the height of the cloud**.

S Yeah, I'd agree with that.

A Oh, right. But then we've also got 'strong', 'moderate' and 'weak' … I'm not sure. Could that be force, do you think?

S I wouldn't have thought so, no. That'll be **the volume of the cloud**. How large it is, basically. The bigger it is, the more likelihood there is of an eruption.

A Yes, that makes sense. Now moving down, we've got something labelled 'dome growth'. Dome, that's the top of the volcano?

S Right.

A Mm. And then 'ashfall'. Which is … ?

S See those little spots? I think you get particles of ash raining down.

A From the cloud, I see. Then up on the slope of the volcano, there's a tree or a bush or something …

S Yes, that'll be **drying vegetation**. As I remember, volcanoes give off an enormous amount of heat before they erupt, and that causes plants and trees and things to dry.

A I'm impressed. How do you remember all this stuff?

S Just my natural brilliance.

A Yeah, right. And then … what's that thing that looks like a hole in the slope?

S I think it's meant to show **a landslide**.

A Really? I'll have to take your word for that! I suppose it's not that easy to illustrate. OK, **landslide it is**. And then we've got, yes, must be rain …

S Well done!

A Thanks! … And a river of some kind. Would it be a river of lava? No, no, not before an eruption, surely?

S No, I think you'll find that's **mudflow**.

A Do you write that as one word or two?

S **Mudflow**. One word. They can happen before a volcanic eruption, as well as during, and if I remember rightly, they can travel at anything up to one hundred kilometres an hour.

A Wow! Really? You wouldn't want to get in the way of one of those, would you? OK, now what about these two little houses … They seem to be shaking. That's got to be **an earthquake**, right? Do you get earthquakes at the same time as volcanoes?

S Uh huh, I think the two things are very often linked, in fact.

A Right. Then there are things like, well, like little flowerpots … and a sign saying 'no water'. I guess they're wells. So, **wells … drying up**! What do you think?

S Yup, sounds about right for that one.

A Next there's a horse which looks as if it's going a bit crazy.

S Yes, that's a very interesting phenomenon. Apparently some animals can sense when there's a disaster coming, and they behave in strange ways. Dogs start barking, geese fly into trees, things like that. I think we can call it **'abnormal animal behaviour'**.

A Yeah, I remember reading about something like that in Japan. **Abnormal animal behaviour**. Got that. OK, next there are obviously some unusual sounds to listen out for.

S   Mm, before an eruption, you get **a rumbling sound**. Like thunder.

A   Thunder's bad enough – a volcano rumbling must be absolutely terrifying! Right, only one left now. And that's to do with smell, right? Quite an unpleasant smell, by the look of it.

S   Yes, volcanoes give off various gases, and one of the most obvious warning signs is **a sulphur smell**. It's pretty unmistakable.

A   **Sulphur**, phew, nasty. OK, well, I think that's it finally. Fantastic. You've been a great help, Sarah. Thanks a million.

S   No problem. But I'd better fly or I'll be late. Good luck with the assignment.

Unit 10, Focus on listening 2
Tsunami (p.101)

Good morning. Today we're going to look at natural hazards connected with the oceans. As you know, more than two-thirds of the Earth's surface is covered by water, and the main hazards, both at sea and along the shore, are caused by waves.

Now, waves can be measured in various ways. So first of all I'd like to clarify a few of the terms we need to use. If you could just turn to the diagram on page 82.

Right? Now, you see the waves running across the centre? And the sea floor at the bottom? OK. Well, **the highest point of a wave is called the 'crest'**. Remember the saying 'to be on the crest of a wave', to be very successful? Yeah? Then an important measurement: **wavelength, which is the distance between the highest point of one wave and the next**. Wavelengths can vary enormously, from a few metres to hundreds of kilometres, believe it or not. So far, so good. What else? Er, there's wave period, which isn't marked because it's a measurement of time. It's the time between one wave crest passing and the next. Then **the lowest point of a wave is known as the 'trough'**. Can you see that? That leaves wave height, which is a measurement of the vertical distance between the crest of a wave and the trough. And finally, depth, which, as I'm sure you know, is the distance between the mean sea level and the sea bed.

Right, well, most waves are produced by the effect of wind. But the most destructive waves of all are not, in fact, wind generated. These are the famous tsunami. The word 'tsunami', by the way, is Japanese for 'harbour wave'. **The majority of tsunami are caused by earthquakes** which occur under the sea bed, although a few are also caused by underwater volcanic eruptions.

Most tsunami – that's between 80 and 90 per cent – take place in the Pacific Ocean. This is because the majority of the Earth's earthquakes happen around that ocean in the so-called 'Ring of Fire'. **While they're in the open sea, tsunami waves are generally quite small, rarely more than half a metre high, in fact**. That usually surprises people. It's only when they reach the shore that tsunami waves reach such enormous heights. As a matter of interest, **the largest tsunami ever recorded was 64 metres high, that was in Russia** in 1737. It's also worth noting that tsunami have extremely long wavelengths. **In the Pacific Ocean, for example, the average wavelength is 480km**. This low height and long wavelength makes it difficult to detect a tsunami in the open sea. The deeper the water, the faster the tsunami travels, and in the Pacific, **they can reach speeds of up to 700km an hour**. In 1960, a tsunami generated by an earthquake in Chile reached Japan in only 22 hours.

Let's look at another example now, the 1964 tsunami which hit Crescent City in the far north of California. This was caused by an earthquake which happened in Alaska four and a half hours earlier. The first two waves only hit the area around the harbour, but the third washed inland for a distance of 500 metres. **It flooded 30 city blocks** and destroyed a number of small, one-storey buildings. Luckily, there'd been enough warning for people to evacuate the low-lying areas, close to the sea shore. But the city authorities learnt an important lesson, and they took steps to prevent the worst of the damage from happening again. They turned the main risk area into a public park, and relocated all the businesses on higher ground. Incidentally, this approach has also been taken in Hawaii and Japan.

Now, before we finish, I'd just like to look at one more hazard, storm surges …

Unit 12, Focus on listening 1
The golden rules of listening (p.120)

P = Presenter; F = Frances Stephens

P   … and now it's time for the first in a new series called 'Get the Message', which looks at communication skills and how to improve them. Here's Frances Stephens to present it.

F   Hello. I think we'd all agree that good communication is vital, whether it's at home, at work or in personal relationships. So what are the key communication skills and how can we improve them? I'll be trying to answer those questions over the next four weeks. We'll be looking at the skill of speaking and considering **how to express yourself clearly in a discussion**, for example, or how to make a good impression in a job interview. We'll also be thinking about writing, including how to write an effective letter of complaint and the uses and abuses of email. And finally, we'll be examining gestures and other **aspects** of **body language**, and considering the effect this has on face-to-face communication. But today, I'm going to start by focusing on the skill of listening.

F Now, listening is a far more sophisticated skill than most people realise, and poor listening is a very common cause of breakdowns in communication, so you need to be aware of a few rules.

The first golden rule of listening is to stop talking. Because you can't listen carefully if you keep interrupting. **This is especially important when the situation is familiar**, when you're talking to a relative or friend, say. In situations like that, it's all too easy to assume you know what the person means and start working out your reply, instead of paying attention to what they're really saying!

Next, try to relax! Research has shown that **it's much more difficult to listen effectively if you're feeling at all tense and anxious**. So if you've been dealing with a tricky problem at work, for example, and you feel the tension building up, take a deep breath before you answer the telephone. Let your brain adjust first.

You also need to make the speaker feel relaxed, and the way to do that is to **show them they have your full attention**. Try to look interested in what they're saying. Don't look over their shoulder or start scribbling on a piece of paper. Of course, **there may be reasons why you want to make notes**. In this case, tell the speaker in advance and explain the reason. Say the notes are to help you remember exactly what they said. Blame your poor memory, if you like. This is important, because we often use facial expression to tell us how the conversation is going.

Next, be aware of any prejudices you have – personal, political, whatever. And **make a conscious effort not to let these views affect your judgement**. You may not see things in exactly the same way as the other person, but that shouldn't stop you from trying to understand their point of view.

It's important to realise that listening is an active process. To listen effectively, **you need to use not only reason, but also feeling**. That means trying to identify with the other person and putting yourself in their position. After all, **the point of listening is to understand the other person's point of view – not to win an argument**. If you can empathise with the speaker, you're much less likely to jump to the wrong conclusion.

And one final point: **remember to listen for what the speaker is *not* saying**. That sounds strange, I know, but very often what's missing from a conversation is at least as important as what's there.

Now, to discuss some of these points, I've got with me in the studio Brian Morgan, who's a psychologist, and Tessa Wade, who works as a marriage guidance counsellor for …

Unit 12, Focus on listening 2
Making the most of your memory (p.121)

Now, today we're looking at memory. How it operates, and how *you* can make the most of it. That's if I remembered to bring my notes with me. They're here somewhere … Don't worry, just kidding!

OK, let's take a look at how memory works. In order for you to remember something, your brain has to perform a number of operations. First, the information has to be encoded, that is, taken in and processed. Then the information has to be held until it's needed, which is **the storage system of the brain**. Finally, it needs to be retrieved so that it can be used.

Most of us have problems with our memory at some time or other, and the older you are, the more likely this is to happen. Exactly how your memory suffers depends on which of your brain's systems is most vulnerable.

Another distinction we have to draw is between **verbal** and visual memory. Think about finding your way in a strange town. You may prefer to take in information verbally, for example, 'Turn left at the cathedral', etc. On the other hand, you may absorb information better in the form of a mental picture. To make the most of your memory, you need to use all these different systems to the full.

Another way of improving memory is with a method known as PQRST. This is a way of linking something you're trying to learn to what you already know. In this method, the P stands for **'Preview'**, that is, glancing through the text before reading it carefully. Then Q for 'Question', R for 'Read' and S … anyone care to hazard a guess? Well, it stands for **'State'**, as in 'to make a statement'. And lastly, the T stands for 'Test'.

OK. Well, let's look at those five steps a little more closely. If you've got an article, say, to read, **the first thing to do is to look through it quickly**, without worrying about every word. And when you've done that, you have to ask yourself, 'What do I know about this topic already?' Only then should you read the article carefully. And when you've done that, you need to **review the contents**. That means thinking about how the contents relate to what you already know about the subject. Finally, you should make a habit of testing yourself about what you've read.

The brain also has another type of memory system, which is called 'implicit memory', and **this enables us to absorb information without paying attention to it**. Sounds good, doesn't it? But there's a catch. If this system is to work efficiently, **it's crucial that you don't make any mistakes** while you're learning. If you're trying to learn a long list of vocabulary, for example, you may guess a few wrong meanings, and then your memory is likely to end up holding on to those wrong meanings.

So, **the best approach is to only test yourself on what you know well**. If you learn a few words at a time and gradually build up the list, you'll learn better than if you try to learn 200 words all at once. Little and often is the rule.

Now, here's something that might interest you. There's been some research in California which suggests that living a life of luxury can make you more intelligent! Scientists divided a group of 24 mice into two groups. One group was kept in standard conditions with as much food and water as they wanted. The other group was kept in luxury with larger cages, comfortable bedding and tasty snacks. And after 40 days, **this second group of mice were found to have fifteen per cent more cell matter in the part of the brain that deals with learning and memory**. Makes you think, doesn't it?

So I'd suggest you go out and pamper yourself a bit before the exams! But seriously, I'd like now to look at some other research into the mechanisms of learning and memory …

Unit 14, Focus on listening 1
Media survey (p.140)

I = Interviewer; P = Philip Matthews

I Excuse me, have you got a few minutes to answer some questions?

P What about?

I I'm doing a survey about how people use the media, things like newspapers, television, computers, etc.

P I see. Well, OK.

I Can I start by taking a few personal details? Don't worry, it's completely confidential.

P Sure.

I First, could I have your name?

P Yes, Philip **Matthews**. That's **M-A-double-T-H-E-W-S**.

I **Matthews**. Right. Got it. And do you mind if I ask your age?

P No, that's all right. **I'm 21** – I'll be 22 next week, as it happens.

I Oh, many happy returns in advance!

P Thanks.

I And what's your occupation?

P I suppose I'd have to say **full-time student**. Is that an occupation?

I It certainly is! OK, now turning to the survey proper. Do you buy a daily paper?

P No. I usually get one on Saturdays, though.

I What's the first thing you turn to in the newspaper?

P That's easy, **the sports section**. Doesn't everyone? You've got to check on your team's progress, read the match report, haven't you? And after that, I generally have a quick look at the **news**.

I When you say 'news', is that local, national or international?

P Oh, I'd say **national news**. Not local. Nothing very exciting happens round here! And I'm not terribly up on international affairs.

I And are there any other sections you read regularly? Business, for example?

P No. You must be joking! Business bores me stiff, I'm afraid. Let me think. I might have a look at the Arts section once in a while, but not as a regular thing. I suppose the only other thing I make a point of looking at is the **TV reviews**.

I You watch a lot of TV?

P 'Fraid I do, yes. Too much, probably!

I Right. That's it for that section …

I Well, if we could turn to TV and radio now …

P Right.

I Is there any particular kind of TV programme you watch?

P Well, the news, obviously, and sport. **But mostly, I want to be entertained. I like a good TV drama.** Something with a strong plot that you can get involved in. I don't watch a lot of documentaries, to be honest, and most of the comedies and quiz shows – they leave me cold.

I And do you listen to the radio at all?

P In the mornings I do. I prefer it to breakfast TV. But that's about the only time.

I So **would you say you got most of your information from television**?

P **Yes, I suppose I would.** As I said, I don't go in for a daily paper.

I And finally, just a couple more questions. Do you use a computer?

P Yes.

I And what would you say you use it for mostly?

P Mm, that's a hard one. I mean, I use it for computer games, like everyone else. But I've been cutting down on that lately. I think at the moment **I probably use it most for typing up lecture notes and other coursework, like assignments**. I did once try to keep an account of my spending on it. But I didn't get very far.

I Do you have internet access?

P Yes.

I How do you use that mainly?

P Well, it can be very useful for college work. I've found an awful lot of information surfing the Web. But **in answer to your question, I think I'd have to say email**. It's just a great way of keeping in touch with friends, especially the ones I have abroad.

I How about online banking? Have you thought about that?

P Not while I've got an overdraft, no!

I Fair enough. OK, well, thanks very much for your time.

P Is that it?

I Yup. That's it.

P OK, well, cheers.

Unit 14, Focus on listening 2
Couch potatoes, (p.141)

T = Tutor; A = Amy; J = Jonathan

T Hi, Amy, Jonathan. Do sit down … OK, we're talking about the media today, and I think Amy, you were going to start us off …

A Yes. I found a couple of pieces of information on the internet.

T Fine.

A OK, well one was a survey of television viewing habits, looking at heavy viewers in different countries …

T And a 'heavy viewer' is … ?

A Yes, sorry. It's someone who watches TV for more than two hours a day. Anyway, there were two countries where more than 50 per cent of the people were heavy viewers. The UK came top with 58 per cent, and **New Zealand wasn't far behind with 53 per cent**. Some of the other results were quite surprising, actually.

T For example?

A Well, I would have expected the USA to be high on the list, but it came quite far down, with 40 per cent. Other countries, like Germany, were much higher. And then **the country with fewest heavy viewers turned out to be Switzerland**. I would have guessed, maybe, Portugal.

T Thanks. Well, that's useful data. Anything else to report?

A Yes, I also found a breakdown of TV programmes shown in an average week. It's only for one channel, but it's probably fairly typical. There are basically two major areas which account for most of the time. One is news stroke factual …

T Sorry, what do you mean by factual?

A Documentaries, current affairs, things like that. And the other is drama stroke entertainment.

T OK.

A Well, **news and factual programmes take up just over a quarter of the week. But drama and entertainment is much more popular. That accounts for about half the week's viewing. And the remaining time – what's that? About another quarter, I suppose – is all the other things like sport, education, the arts, etc.**

T OK. You might want to try and get data for one or two other countries perhaps. Anyway, thanks for that, Amy. Now, Jonathan, over to you …

J OK, well, I was interested in how children use the media, and I thought I'd look at the kind of home entertainment equipment children have access to.

T That's an interesting angle. What equipment specifically?

J Basically, video recorders, CD players and satellite TV.

T Right.

J Well, **video recorders seem to be pretty well universal nowadays. Almost every home with children has one, and that's been the case for at least ten years.** On the other hand, **CD players used to be a lot less common, but there's been a steady increase in recent years, and now about two-thirds of families have one.** Then finally, **satellite TV – that was fairly rare to begin with, but again there's been a gradual increase and nowadays it's in about a quarter of homes with children.**

T That's useful data, good.

T OK, Jonathan, now what would you say is the most important medium for children?

J TV, definitely.

T Any thoughts about why that should be?

J Well, I suppose television offers a lot of things: excitement, relaxation, etc. And it doesn't make any demands. It's a passive activity. But probably **mostly because all their friends watch it, and they don't want to feel left out**.

T Good point. Amy, you have a question?

A Yes, do we know how much time children spend watching TV?

J I think it's about two and a half hours a day in Britain, more than most other European countries, anyway. I remember another surprising statistic was that **two out of three children in Britain have TVs in their bedroom**.

A Really, as many as that?

J Yes, but the good thing is … is that their parents know where they are.

A But not necessarily what they're watching!

T Jonathan, any idea how many children have access to a computer?

J Just a sec. Yes, in Britain at any rate, 53% of children have a computer in the home. But **only about a quarter have a computer actually in their bedroom.**

T Mm. That's still quite a significant proportion, though. Anyway, finally, did either of you consider books at all? Or are they just old hat these days?

A Well, judging by the kids I know, I'd say books were definitely out of favour. They seem to see books as **dull and boring**. The sort of thing your parents approve of, you know. **Not exactly fashionable** amongst your friends!

J Yeah, my younger brothers are the same. Reading books is **too much like hard work** compared with watching TV. If they want entertainment, they'd definitely watch TV rather than read a book.

T What a shame! Well, all you need to do now is to write a report on your findings. By the end of next week, OK?

Unit 16, Focus on listening 1
Reality or science fiction? (p.160)

J = Jack; H = Helen

J Hello?

H Jack? It's Helen here. Look, this is just a quick call. I've found an article on the internet that might be useful for that assignment you're doing. It's basically a science-fiction writer's predictions about the future.

J Great – I could do with some inspiration!

H Well, if you've got something to write with, I can run through them for you.

J Just a sec … Right, go ahead.

H OK. Well, the first prediction is **'Massive, rapid change'**. He says **it's going to affect just about every area of life, political, social, economic and so on**. That's in the first category, which he calls 'Definite'.

J So he's put the predictions in categories. Interesting. But does he mention any specific causes?

H Let me see … Yes. He says **the transformations will be driven by**, and I quote, '**the forces of demography**, which has incredible mass, **and technology**, which has incredible velocity'.

J I'm writing that down. Right.

H Right. There are three more in the 'Definite' section: 'More city dwellers' …

J I've got a lot on that already, actually, but tell me about the other two.

H OK, well, talking about animals, he says that at the moment **more species are being destroyed than are coming into existence**.

J Species … Yup. Got that. Next?

H And on languages, he says **there are about 6,000 spoken today. But about half of those aren't being taught in school any more, so they're bound to die out.**

J I must say I didn't realise it was as many as that.

H No. Anyway, the next category is 'Almost certain'. You've probably got most of these: 'Global warming … computers everywhere …'

J Yes, got those.

H … 'more people' …

J Yes, population explosion, etc. But just a sec. He doesn't give any up-to-date figure for global population, does he?

H I think so. Yes. Six billion – that was the figure for 2000, at any rate. He also asks the question 'How many people can the Earth support?' Apparently, **most estimates put the Earth's long-term capacity at four to six billion**.

J But we've reached that already!

H I know, scary isn't it? Anyway, the third category is 'Probable', and here we've got 'More countries' …

J That can't be right, can it?

H Well, he says **there's a trend towards more and smaller countries which is going to continue**. He points out that the Soviet Union broke into fifteen parts.

J Right.

H … 'longer lives' …

J Got that.

H … and the other one here is 'Alternative energy'.

J Go on.

H He says **the basic science and engineering for a new energy economy will be completed by 2025**. But he thinks it'll probably take most of the century for it to actually be implemented worldwide.

J I'm just scribbling that down … OK, next?

H 'Space exploration'. He says **the exploration of our solar system will continue**, with more probes, more satellites, etc. **But only as long as we have political stability.**

J Good point. I'd better mention that – 'political stability – key factor'. Right.

H And he also thinks **new countries will be involved. He mentions China, Japan and Korea.** OK?

J OK.

H Then the last category is 'Possible' with only two headings. One is 'Nuclear war' …

J So he's not optimistic about world peace?

H Not terribly. He mentions several causes for concern. Like the amount of nuclear know-how there is around these days. And the fact that **there are still so many problem situations in different parts of the world, which could end up in conflict**. But also just the sheer number of nuclear weapons in existence.

J How depressing.

H And then the last prediction is what he calls 'First contact', finding life on other planets, I suppose.

J I think I'll steer clear of science fiction. Anyway, all this has been a huge help. Thanks a billion, Helen.

H No problem. Bye.

J Bye.

Unit 16, Focus on listening 2
The techno-house (p.161)

Next, as part of our Continuing Education series, we take a look at the house of the future. In recent years, house builders have been keen to show the public what new homes could look like. And to demonstrate what's possible, they've built special show homes featuring all the latest technology and energy-saving features.

But although the technology is already in place to bring all these exciting innovations into people's living rooms and bedrooms, very few new houses actually include them. Why is this? Well, it seems that **public demand for the house of the future is still very low**.

It seems people are not terribly interested in environmentally friendly technology. According to the developers, the home buyer's first consideration is price. They're simply not willing to pay extra for the benefit of all the latest technology. After price, **the thing they're most concerned about is location**. They may want to be near a good school, for example, or close to the shops. The third main consideration is design. And it seems most buyers still want to live in a traditional-looking house.

That said, there are a few forward-looking designers around who are hoping to persuade British people to abandon their prejudices and choose something new. A group called the Integer Project is designing houses which are both intelligent and green. For them, state-of-the-art design doesn't have to mean expensive. Integer Project houses use lightweight materials and prefabricated panels, which save both time and money. A typical three-storey house will take only 28 weeks to build, and that's **a saving of 20 weeks on conventional construction.**

One of the buildings designed by the Integer Project is the so-called Millennium House. This incorporates a whole host of high-tech energy-saving features, including computer-controlled energy-efficient lighting and heating. But one of its most unusual features has to be **the roof, which is covered with grass**. This provides an effective form of insulation, but how you manage to cut it, I'm not sure! The building is actually designed as a house within a house. There's an inner box containing all the main rooms, and this is **surrounded by an outer glasshouse**, which provides a controlled climate where plants can be grown. The lower floor is below ground level, so it's sheltered by earth on three sides to prevent heat loss. And outside, **the water is collected from the roof in a pond**. The water from the pond can then be used for watering the garden, and there's also equipment for recycling organic waste.

Integer principles are actually being tried out in one house in a new development by Berkeley Homes. Here, heating and lighting are controlled by computers, and the water is recycled within the house. **Water for domestic purposes can also be heated by solar energy**, thanks to solar panels fitted on the roof. This house is going to be the subject of ongoing research as to the benefits of its design and construction.

Another developer, Laing Homes, has teamed up with a firm of internet experts to build a five-bedroom show house near London, which is called **the 'Internet House'**. From the outside, the house looks much like any other family home. But inside is a fascinating computer brain. The technology also allows a homeowner **to operate the heating, the TV, the security system and even the garden watering from the office or car using a website**.

A third developer, Redrow Homes, has taken the brave step of building 'The House for the Future', which can be seen at the Museum of Welsh Life near Cardiff. The most unusual design feature here is that **the staircase can be moved**. By changing the position of the staircase, you can alter the shape and size of the rooms as the family grows, and lifestyles change. The house is also extremely environmentally friendly, with facilities for recycling both water and waste.

'The House for the Future' provides a fascinating glimpse of what the future holds. The museum is open Monday to Friday …

Unit 18, Focus on listening 1
Worldwide Student Projects (p.180)

Hi, everyone. My name's Sam Thomas, and I'm here to give you some information about Worldwide Student Projects, or WSP for short. The talk takes about five minutes, and after that I'll be happy to answer questions, OK?

Right, well, WSP is a voluntary service organisation, which was **set up to promote international understanding**. Right now, we've got people from 30 different countries working in local communities around the world. So, if you're interested in joining them, I'd like to tell you about some of the opportunities that are available.

Now, depending how long you want to be away, there are three sorts of project to choose from: short-term projects lasting two to three weeks, medium-term projects lasting between one and six months and long-term projects which can be anything up to a year. One of the short-term ones we've got on offer at the moment is in Japan. **It's a village improvement project**, and the work involves clearing the river banks and planting flowers, things like that. You'd be working alongside local people, so **you need a basic knowledge of Japanese for that.**

The next one to tell you about is a **children's holiday centre in Poland**. What's required here is basically manual work. You'll be painting rooms, gardening and generally preparing for the children's arrival. It's a medium-term project lasting six weeks, and there's comfortable accommodation on site.

And now something for the animal lovers amongst you. It's a conservation project for sea turtles in Mexico. Sea turtles are under threat from poachers in that part of the world, so your main job would be collecting and moving the eggs to a safe site. It's a short-term project, and you'd be staying in a local school, but be aware that **it has very basic conditions**. Don't expect any luxury or satellite TV!

Now, here's an exciting opportunity in China for any budding architects. This is a long-term project, and placements are for nine months. You'd be working in an office in Shanghai, involved in planning and design, under supervision of a local architect. Oh, and I should mention that **you have to pay an additional fee of 250 US dollars when you arrive.**

Finally, do we have any medical students here? Because there's a placement available in **a centre for disabled children in India**. You'd be providing general medical care and also assisting in the outpatients department. It's for six months, so you can get plenty of experience and also do something worthwhile for disabled children.

Well, that's just a taste of the incredible range of projects we have to offer, but I hope it's whetted your appetite. And in case you do decide to apply, let me tell you what happens next.

First of all, you need to fill in an application form and send it to us. Oh, and **you should also include a passport photo**, by the way. Once we've received the form and photo, we process them and then we send you a 'Welcome' pack containing general information about the programme, together with the **formal terms and conditions**. These **terms and conditions** are basically a list of responsibilities on both sides, yours and ours – what happens if you want to leave early, etc. And you also get a detailed questionnaire, which helps us identify a suitable job for you.

Then, **about one month before you leave,** you'll receive all the details about your particular placement. And I think that's about it. Oh, I nearly forgot to mention, we've also got a website. The address is in our brochure. Now, are there any questions?

Unit 18, Focus on listening 2
The end of oil (p.183)

T = Tutor; A = Andrew

T Well, as I say, Andrew, we were a bit worried about your progress last term, but you've done some very good work recently, and I think it's fairly safe to assume you'll pass the course now. **In fact, if you can keep up this standard, we could very well be looking at a Credit.**

A **A Credit?** Really?

T Yes, as long as you keep up the good work. It's a real pity about last term, because you could have got a Distinction if you'd really wanted to, you know. Anyway, the other thing we need to talk about is your next assignment, right?

A Right.

T And you wanted to look at the subject of oil.

A Yes, it's a pretty major issue. I mean, there are millions of buses and cars and trucks in the world, all dependent on oil, and then the airline industry is carrying more and more people around the world every year, so you have to consider global warming …

T Hang on a minute, **I wouldn't go into global warming if I were you**. That's a huge subject in its own right, and quite a controversial one, I might add. **The assignment is only supposed to be 3,000 words**, remember. If you're not careful, you'll be writing a 30,000-word thesis!

A OK.

T Don't be too ambitious and keep an eye on the number of words. You've got a word count on your computer, haven't you?

A Yes.

T Good. Now, let's start with a few basics. Do you know how much energy is actually used for fuel, compared with other things?

A Yes, I found a breakdown. It's here somewhere … ah, yes, **transportation, that accounts for about a quarter of world energy**. Quite a bit less than industry, but it's still a significant proportion.

T **And what is the figure for industry**, as a matter of interest?

A **That's almost 45 per cent.**

T And the rest?

A **The other 30 per cent or so goes into buildings**, for things like heating and air conditioning, etc. But anyway, the main point I wanted to make was that we can't go on relying on oil for ever.

T So, Andrew, you think oil is running out. Have you any evidence of that?

A Yes, and it's quite frightening. Apparently, nowadays oil companies are only finding one barrel of oil for every four we actually use. Britain's North Sea oil is just about at its peak now. It'll start to decline pretty soon. And several major oil producers are already producing less …

T For example?

A Well, **the former Soviet Union is** a good example, and **Mexico** is another. Apparently even Saudi Arabia will reach its peak in a few more years.

T Interesting. OK, and do you know which countries use the most oil?

A Yes, a third of all the world's oil goes to North America. Worst of all is **the USA**, which gets through 459 gallons of gasoline per head every year, and Canada isn't far behind, with 303 gallons. Quite a long way after that comes **Germany** and then **Japan**.

T All fairly predictable, I suppose.

A Mm. But the thing is, there are other countries catching up fast, especially in the Asia-Pacific region. The two fastest growing are **South Korea**, which has doubled its use of gasoline in ten years, and **India**, which is up 64% in the same period.

T Good, that's all very useful data. Now, I suppose the other thing you need to look at is possible solutions. Any ideas?

A I haven't really got that far yet …

T OK, well, it comes down to two or three things, doesn't it? Persuading people to use less oil …

A By putting a tax on it, you mean. But that can penalise the poor.

T … or discovering new oil reserves somewhere in the world.

A Unlikely, and even that would only be a stop-gap. No, **I think the only realistic long-term answer is to find a replacement for oil**. I've seen hydrogen mentioned as a likely candidate.

T OK, well, I think we'd better leave it there. You seem to have a lot of useful information already, and you just need to work out the last section. And don't forget the word limit!

A I won't. Thanks for the help.

Unit 20, Focus on listening 1
Photography courses (p.199)

W = woman; M = man

W Department of Art, Design and Media. Can I help you?

M Yes. I'd like some information about photography courses.

W Let me just get the prospectus … OK, well, we do several different courses. I'll just run through them for you. The first is 'Introducing photography'. That runs for ten weeks and **it's a Foundation-level course**, so it's for people just beginning in photography.

M Right.

W That's on Monday evenings, from six thirty to nine thirty. Next, there's **'Black and white photography', which is at Intermediate level**, so you would need some previous experience for that one. And you also have to have an interview with a tutor beforehand.

M Sounds interesting. Which evening is it on?

W It's a daytime course, actually. **From two to four thirty** on Tuesdays. That's also for ten weeks.

M That's a pity, I work on Tuesday afternoons.

W There's also 'Landscape photography', which is on Tuesday evenings, from six thirty to nine. That's a longer course than the others, **it runs for sixteen weeks**.

M And do you need previous experience for that one?

W Let me just check … Mm, it's Advanced level. So yes, you would, yes, and again you'd have to be interviewed beforehand. OK? Then the only other one we do is 'The art of digital photography'.

M I'm not sure that's for me, but which evening is it?

W **It's a flexitime course.** It's on a Wednesday, but **you can do it at any time to suit you during the day**.

M How many weeks is that?

W It's up to you, really. **You have to do 60 hours in all.** And again, there's an interview.

M Right.

M OK. Can I just go back to the first course you mentioned. Um, what sort of things does that cover?

W 'Introducing photography'? Let's see what it says in the prospectus. Yes, here it is: 'Find out about different types of camera and camera care, **learn how the camera's controls operate**, and which lenses to use for different subjects, **study the main elements of effective composition'**. That's all it says. You could always talk to the tutor if you wanted more information.

M It sounds a bit … basic, to be honest. What about 'Landscape photography', was that the next one?

W Yes, that includes a field trip, where you go out with your tutor on location. But, look, to save me reading everything out, why don't I send you the prospectus?

M That'd be great. But could you just give me an idea of the fees?

W I'll just have to check … Right, 'Introducing photography', that's … yes, £95. 'Black and white's the same, I think … No, I tell a lie, it's a bit less, actually, **£85**. And then 'Landscape' and 'Digital', they're both £140.

M Gosh. That's a bit steep, isn't it?

W Well, they are longer courses, if you remember. With the 'Digital', the fee also includes some photographic materials. And with the 'Landscape', **the cost of that field trip I mentioned is included**.

M Right. Oh, and I forgot to ask, is there an examination?

W Not as such. But you can have your work assessed and get a certificate if you pay a small extra fee.

M I see. Just one last question. How soon would I need to apply?

W Well, there are still places on all the courses at the moment, but they do tend to fill up quickly. 'Introducing photography' is always popular – we're running two courses this year so we can meet the demand. And 'Digital' is getting quite popular, too. But **there are only twelve places on the 'Black and white' course**, so that everyone has access to the equipment. **If you're interested in applying for that one, I wouldn't leave it too long, if I were you**.

M I'll bear that in mind. Thanks very much for your help.

Unit 20, Focus on listening 2
History of cinema (p.200)

Right, if everyone's here … What I'd like to do in this first session of the Film Studies module is to take a brief look at the development of cinematography and pick out a few landmarks along the way. OK?

Now, the history of moving pictures begins with the camera, obviously. And the history of the camera goes way back to the 11th century, and something called the 'camera obscura', which was used in Arabia for observing solar eclipses. Over the centuries, **the camera-obscura principle was developed into a tool for drawing**. But this had serious limitations as a camera, because there was no way of actually fixing the image.

Then from the 17th century, we have the so-called 'magic lantern', which is really the forerunner of today's film projector. This began life as a way of showing scientific pictures, but because it could tell a story, **the magic lantern became most widely used for the purposes of entertainment**, and in the 19th century some very elaborate and expensive models were developed.

The first instrument which showed naturally moving pictures was the so-called 'Kinetoscope', nicknamed the 'peep-hole machine', and this was patented by Thomas Edison in 1894. The disadvantage with this was that **the film could only be seen by one person at a time**. So, although it was a great step forward, the Kinetoscope never achieved great popularity.

And then, around the year 1895, we reach the beginning of cinematography proper. It was in that year that **the Lumière brothers showed off the world's first projection system** to an audience in Paris. Incidentally, the film they screened with the new system showed a train approaching a station, and apparently it was so realistic that some of the audience ran out of the building in terror. All the same, the movies had been born.

As time went on, directors experimented with different kinds of film. One of the biggest successes of the early years was also **the first Western film ever made. This was a film called *The Great Train Robbery***, shot in 1903, and it paved the way for the careers of the great cowboy heroes like John Wayne.

As you know, the early films were silent, and usually accompanied by piano music. There were a few short experimental sound films during the early twenties, but **it wasn't until 1927 that the first full-length sound film was produced. This was the famous *The Jazz Singer***, starring Al Jolson. At first, the film industry saw sound in films as just a gimmick which wouldn't last, but *The Jazz Singer* was so successful, they had to think again.

The final piece of the jigsaw was the arrival of Technicolor. **This was first seen in a cartoon made by Disney in 1932.** However, colour movies were expensive and difficult to produce, and it was 30 years or so before they completely replaced black and white.

Now, a word about the studios. The American film industry originally grew up on the east coast, in New York and Philadelphia. But filmmakers needed more reliable weather, and in 1910, many of them headed west for California. Now, why California? Well, apart from all-year-round sunshine, they found **plenty of cheap land** available where they could create studios and build houses. Another attraction was **the low wages** for all the various workers they needed to make films. And California also offered **incredibly varied landscapes** for every type of movie.

So directors and film stars poured into the little town of Hollywood, and the population expanded by an incredible 700 per cent in just ten years. And in no time at all, the name 'Hollywood' meant just one thing: movies.

Photocopiable Activities

Unit 1 *Personally speaking ...*

Are you the kind of person who likes to exercise regularly, or do you prefer to relax and take things easy?	Do you think it's important to take regular exercise?	What are the advantages and disadvantages of spending a lot of time exercising?
Er ... / Um ... ☐☐ You know, ... ☐☐ Pause (5 seconds or more) ☐☐ Repetition ☐☐	Er ... / Um ... ☐☐ You know, ... ☐☐ Pause (5 seconds or more) ☐☐ Repetition ☐☐	Er ... / Um ... ☐☐ You know, ... ☐☐ Pause (5 seconds or more) ☐☐ Repetition ☐☐
In your opinion, do you think young people get less exercise now than they used to?	What, in your opinion, are the best ways of staying fit and healthy?	What are the best ways of encouraging young people to take more exercise?
Er ... / Um ... ☐☐ You know, ... ☐☐ Pause (5 seconds or more) ☐☐ Repetition ☐☐	Er ... / Um ... ☐☐ You know, ... ☐☐ Pause (5 seconds or more) ☐☐ Repetition ☐☐	Er ... / Um ... ☐☐ You know, ... ☐☐ Pause (5 seconds or more) ☐☐ Repetition ☐☐
Do you think that people worry too much about eating the wrong kinds of food and not getting enough exercise?	What advice would you give to someone who decided they were unfit and unhealthy and wanted to change their lifestyle?	Do you enjoy playing sport? Why/Why not?
Er ... / Um ... ☐☐ You know, ... ☐☐ Pause (5 seconds or more) ☐☐ Repetition ☐☐	Er ... / Um ... ☐☐ You know, ... ☐☐ Pause (5 seconds or more) ☐☐ Repetition ☐☐	Er ... / Um ... ☐☐ You know, ... ☐☐ Pause (5 seconds or more) ☐☐ Repetition ☐☐
Do you think it is possible to remain fit and healthy without taking regular exercise?	It is often said that people in the 21st century are less healthy than they were 100 years ago. Why do you think this might be?	How would you feel if a law was introduced that made everyone take at least an hour of exercise every day?
Er ... / Um ... ☐☐ You know, ... ☐☐ Pause (5 seconds or more) ☐☐ Repetition ☐☐	Er ... / Um ... ☐☐ You know, ... ☐☐ Pause (5 seconds or more) ☐☐ Repetition ☐☐	Er ... / Um ... ☐☐ You know, ... ☐☐ Pause (5 seconds or more) ☐☐ Repetition ☐☐

Unit 2 *Perfect pairs*

In many poorer countries, people bake their own bread, **(1A)** _____ in richer, more developed countries, **(1B)** _____ prefer to get their bread from a supermarket. **(2A)** _____ bread being cheap and easy to make, people prefer the convenience of picking up a ready-made loaf, as **(2B)** _____ as taking advantage of the huge variety of breads on offer. Bread is **(3A)** _____ a common food that many of **(3B)** _____ never consider how it gets to our shops. So if you ever wondered how it happens, here is a brief description.

The ingredients needed to make bread, **(4A)** _____ mainly consist of flour, salt, yeast[1] and oil, are delivered to the factory, **(4B)** _____ the bread-making process begins. **(5A)** _____ of all, **(5B)** _____ flour is mixed with the salt and yeast. Water and oil are **(6A)** _____ added to the mixture **(6B)** _____ stirred to form a thick paste. **(7A)** _____ is then kneaded[2] by hand or by machine to make a dough[3], **(7B)** _____ is cut into small pieces to make individual loaves. In **(8A)** _____ to loaves, **(8B)** _____ may also be used to make other products, such as pizza bases). **(9A)** _____ are all left in a warm, dry room in **(9B)** _____ to allow the dough to rise. The temperature of the room is important, **(10A)** _____ the yeast, **(10B)** _____ makes the dough rise, needs warmth.

(11A) _____ **(11B)** _____ is happening, the oven is heated to about 180°. As **(12A)** _____ as it has reached the correct temperature **(12B)** _____ the loaves are the correct size, they are placed inside and baked for about 35 minutes. **(13A)** _____ brown on the outside and sound hollow when tapped on the bottom, **(13B)** _____ are removed and left to cool. They are almost ready to be delivered to the supermarket, **(14A)** _____ before **(14B)** _____, they must be sliced and packed.

[1] yeast /jiːst/: a substance that is used to make bread rise.
[2] knead /niːd/: to press a mixture of flour and water many times with your hands.
[3] dough /dəʊ/: a mixture of flour, water, etc., used to make bread or pastry.

(A) soon / **(B)** and	**(A)** therefore / **(B)** that
(A) In spite / **(B)** soon	**(A)** order / **(B)** they
(A) While / **(B)** this	**(A)** which / **(B)** where
(A) This / **(B)** which	**(A)** whereas / **(B)** they
(A) then / **(B)** and	**(A)** Before / **(B)** it
(A) thus / **(B)** it	**(A)** When / **(B)** they
(A) These / **(B)** order	**(A)** addition / **(B)** it
(A) Despite / **(B)** well	**(A)** because / **(B)** which
(A) So / **(B)** addition	**(A)** but / **(B)** that
(A) First / **(B)** the	**(A)** such / **(B)** us

Unit 3 *Give us a word*

Team A

(1A) You can find the city between the Black Mountains and the Bay of Tranquility.	**(1B)** The city ____ between the Black Mountains and the Bay of Tranquility.
(2A) Since 1990, more than three million people have poured into the city from the countryside.	**(2B)** Since 1990, more than three million people have ____ ____ the city from the countryside.
(3A) The population exploded in the early 21st century.	**(3B)** The population ____ ____ in the early 21st century.
(4A) The city has more people than any other city in the world.	**(4B)** The city ____ ____ ____ ____ ____ in the world.
(5A) There is really awful overcrowding in the suburbs.	**(5B)** There is ____ overcrowding in the suburbs.
(6A) People think the population is about ten million.	**(6B)** The population ____ ____ ____ ____ about ten million.
(7A) It can be rather tricky finding somewhere to live.	**(7B)** It can be ____ ____ finding somewhere to live.
(8A) Loads of tourists visit the city.	**(8B)** The city is a ____ tourist ____.

Here are the words to give to Team B

accommodation   are   be   been   claimed   famous   for   has   However
increasingly   insufficient   is   is   It   of   result   the   to   Unsurprisingly

--✂---

Team B

(1A) There aren't enough places to live for people moving to the city.	**(1B)** There ____ ____ ____ for people moving to the city.
(2A) Nobody would be surprised to hear the city is badly polluted.	**(2B)** ____, the city is badly polluted.
(3A) The cost of living in the city is becoming more and more expensive.	**(3B)** The cost of living in the city is becoming ____ expensive.
(4A) Everybody knows about the city's beautiful parks and gardens.	**(4B)** The city ____ ____ ____ its beautiful parks and gardens.
(5A) Some people have said that there are more parks here than in any other city in the world.	**(5B)** ____ ____ ____ said that there are more parks here than in any other city in the world.
(6A) Many people say the restaurants in the city are the best in the country.	**(6B)** The restaurants in the city ____ ____ ____ ____ the best in the country.
(7A) There are many restaurants in the city. But they are very expensive.	**(7B)** There are many restaurants in the city. ____, they are very expensive.
(8A) The high prices are down to the high prices restaurant owners have to pay for rent.	**(8B)** The high prices are ____ ____ ____ the high prices restaurant owners have to pay for rent.

Here are the words to give to Team A

be   destination   difficult   estimated   highly   increased   is   is   lies   most   moved
popular   populated   quite   rapidly   severe   the   to   to

Unit 4 *Two cities*

Part 1

Student A

Your city is called Gallio.

Average salary: $22,190

Cost of a burger: $1.20

Average bus fare: $1.50

Cost of a cinema ticket: $1.45

Average electricity bill: $95 per month

Cost of petrol: $2.13 per litre

Rent for a three-room apartment:
$410 per month

Percentage of population living below the poverty line: 23%

Student B

Your city is called Moesia.

Average salary: $22,230

Cost of a burger: $3.60–$4.80

Average bus fare: $1.50

Cost of a cinema ticket: $3

Average electricity bill: $180 per month

Cost of petrol: $2.13 per litre

Rent for a three-room apartment:
$415 per month

Percentage of population living below the poverty line: 27%

✂ -

Part 2

a) There is very _____ difference between average salaries in the two cities. (9)

b) A burger is between _____ and _____ _____ more expensive in Moesia. (5, 4 and 2)

c) An average bus fare costs _____ the same in both cities. (11)

d) A cinema ticket costs _____ _____ _____ as much in Gallio. (12, 1 and 3)

e) Electricity prices are _____ _____ as expensive in Moesia as they are in Gallio. (7 and 13)

f) Petrol prices are _____ in both cities. (8)

g) Rent for a three-room apartment costs _____ the same in both cities. (10)

h) About a _____ of the population of both cities lives below the poverty line. (6)

> It's difficult to _____ between the two cities in terms of population, or the facilities and amenities.

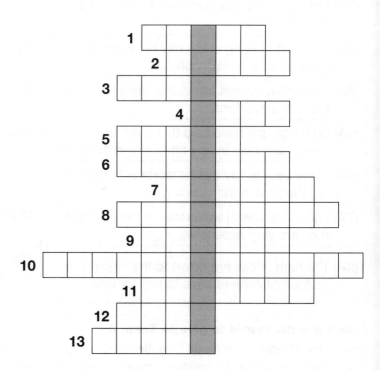

Unit 5 *Top topics*

Group 1: Your topic is **SPORT**

Write four separate sentences about sport. Each sentence should use the word *sport*, but don't write the word – leave a gap.

Write the sentences on a separate sheet of paper.

Each sentence should include a fact or an opinion (see SB p.55 for useful expressions).

Group 2: Your topic is **EDUCATION**

Write four separate sentences about education. Each sentence should use the word *education*, but don't write the word – leave a gap.

Write the sentences on a separate sheet of paper.

Each sentence should include a fact or an opinion (see SB p.55 for useful expressions).

Group 3: Your topic is the **ENVIRONMENT**

Write four separate sentences about the environment. Each sentence should use the word *environment*, but don't write the word – leave a gap.

Write the sentences on a separate sheet of paper.

Each sentence should include a fact or an opinion (see SB p.55 for useful expressions).

Group 4: Your topic is **TECHNOLOGY**

Write four separate sentences about technology. Each sentence should use the word *technology*, but don't write the word – leave a gap.

Write the sentences on a separate sheet of paper.

Each sentence should include a fact or an opinion (see SB p.55 for useful expressions).

Group 5: Your topic is **TRAVEL**

Write four separate sentences about travel. Each sentence should use the word *travel*, but don't write the word – leave a gap.

Write the sentences on a separate sheet of paper.

Each sentence should include a fact or an opinion (see SB p.55 for useful expressions).

Group 6: Your topic is **WORK**

Write four separate sentences about work. Each sentence should use the word *work*, but don't write the word – leave a gap.

Write the sentences on a separate sheet of paper.

Each sentence should include a fact or an opinion (see SB p.55 for useful expressions).

Group 7: Your topic is **CRIME**

Write four separate sentences about crime. Each sentence should use the word *crime*, but don't write the word – leave a gap.

Write the sentences on a separate sheet of paper.

Each sentence should include a fact or an opinion (see SB p.55 for useful expressions).

Group 8: Your topic is **CHILDREN**

Write four separate sentences about children. Each sentence should use the word *children*, but don't write the word – leave a gap.

Write the sentences on a separate sheet of paper.

Each sentence should include a fact or an opinion (see SB p.55 for useful expressions).

Group 9: Your topic is **FOOD**

Write four separate sentences about food. Each sentence should use the word *food*, but don't write the word – leave a gap.

Write the sentences on a separate sheet of paper.

Each sentence should include a fact or an opinion (see SB p.55 for useful expressions).

Group 10: Your topic is **MONEY**

Write four separate sentences about money. Each sentence should use the word *money*, but don't write the word – leave a gap.

Write the sentences on a separate sheet of paper.

Each sentence should include a fact or an opinion (see SB p.55 for useful expressions).

Unit 6 *Silent bingo*

accurate   achieve   activity   administrate   adventurous   alternative
analytical   argument   assign   assist   athletic   aware   benefit   cerebral
challenge   clarify   commence   competitive   conscious   contribute
creative   demonstrate   determined   economy   environment   error   factor
feature   general   initial   institute   intelligent   locate   logical   maximise
obtain   occur   particular   patient   physical   previous   regulate
resource   quiet   scenic   significant   sociable   strategic   unavailable

Game 1

Game 2

Unit 7 *Noun phrase risk*

about   about   agreement   barrier   cost   dependence   discovery   fossil   fuels   hour information   language   living   of   of   of   of   on   our   point   rush   technology the   the   the   view   worry

No.	Sentences	Points risked
1	**(A)** The increasing use of fuels that are produced by the very gradual decay of animals and plants over millions of years is often blamed for global warming. **(B)** The increasing use of _____ is often blamed for global warming.	
2	**(A)** The study or use of electronic processes for gathering and storing information and making it available using computers has come a long way in the last twenty years. **(B)** _____ has come a long way in the last twenty years.	
3	**(A)** During that time of day when the roads, buses, trains, etc. are most full because people are travelling to or from work, it is often quicker to walk. **(B)** During the _____, it is often quicker to walk.	
4	**(A)** Even experienced and confident travellers worry that when they are abroad, the problem of communicating with people who speak a different language may cause problems. **(B)** Even experienced and confident travellers worry that when they are abroad, the _____ may cause problems.	
5	**(A)** Many people would agree that learning a foreign language is difficult. **(B)** There is widespread _____ difficulty of learning a foreign language.	
6	**(A)** Many people were worried that the virus would be extremely severe. **(B)** There was widespread _____ severity of the virus.	
7	**(A)** The amount of money you need to pay for food, clothing, etc. is rising constantly. **(B)** The _____ is rising constantly.	
8	**(A)** Whether or not you think children should have more freedom depends very much on your personal opinion or attitude. **(B)** Whether or not you think children should have more freedom depends very much on your _____.	
9	**(A)** Last year, a scientific journal reported that water had been discovered on Mars. **(B)** Last year, a scientific journal reported _____ water on Mars.	

You begin with 100 points. For each answer that you are **very** sure is correct, you can risk 15 points. For each answer that you are **quite** sure is correct, you can risk 10 points. For each answer that you are **not** sure about, you can risk 5 points. Write the number of points you are prepared to risk for each sentence in the right-hand column.

Unit 8 *In a nutshell*

The destruction of the world's rainforests is the single biggest threat to the environment, and priority should be given to preventing further destruction. Do you agree with this statement?

1
2
3
4
5

It has often been said that, rather than making our lives easier, technology has actually made life more complicated. Would you agree?

1
2
3
4
5

Many people argue that it is cruel and unnecessary to keep animals in zoos, and all animals in zoos should be released into their natural habitat. Do you share this opinion?

1
2
3
4
5

It is generally believed that tourism helps countries and local communities, but some argue that far from benefiting countries, tourism actually does more harm than good. Which do you think is true?

1
2
3
4
5

Young people should be encouraged to spend a year or two travelling around different countries when they finish school or university. Do you think this is a good idea?

1
2
3
4
5

Unit 9 *Double-decker Dominoes*

Start ⇨ **(Top card)**	The number of **academ__** staff declined sharply after 2007.	The protest was a **symbol__** gesture of anger at national environmental policy.	Pollution is often responsible for **respirat__** diseases associated with city living.
Start ⇨ **(Bottom card)**	⇧ Relating to education, especially at college or university level.	⇧ Important, but not having any real effect.	⇧ Relating to breathing or your lungs.
Many **migrat__** routes are being affected by changes to the environment.	Data from the research was interesting but also rather **unreli__**.	The government should do more to promote **sustain__** agriculture.	The techniques used 10 years ago to measure pollution are not **appropri__** now.
⇧ Involved in, or relating to, the movement of animals and birds from one part of the world to another.	⇧ Something that is unable to be trusted or depended on.	⇧ Something that is able to continue without causing damage to the environment.	⇧ Correct or suitable for a particular time, situation or purpose.
The disease spreads quickly in areas where there is **inadequ__** health care.	Only immediate action by the government prevented an **ecologi__** disaster.	Sleep disorders are a serious **psychologi__** problem.	A **vari__** diet is just one factor that affects our health and ability to function well.
⇧ Not good enough, big enough, skilled enough, etc, for a particular purpose.	⇧ Connected with the way plants, animals and people are related to each other and their environment.	⇧ Relating to the way your mind works and the way it affects your behaviour.	⇧ Consisting of or including many different kinds of things.
What the city really needs is an **integrat__** and more reliable public transport system.	The decision to ban cars from the city at weekends was highly **controvers__**.	Cycling and swimming are both believed to be extremely **benefic__** to health.	Rainforests cover 7% of **glob__** landmass.
⇧ Combining many different groups, ideas or parts in a way that works well.	⇧ Causing a lot of disagreement because many people have strong opinions about the subject.	⇧ Having a good effect.	⇧ Affecting or including the whole world.
The **municip__** authorities failed to address local concerns about pollution.	Unemployment in **urb__** areas doubled during the economic crisis.	**Equestri__** sports and events are very popular in my country.	**Finish** **(Top card)**
⇧ Relating to or belonging to the government.	⇧ Relating to towns and cities.	⇧ Relating to horse-riding.	**Finish** **(Bottom card)**

Unit 10 *Total recall*

(A) subsidy	**(B) convene**	**(C) predominant**
(D) analogy	**(E) conceive**	**(F) initial**
(G) framework	**(H) implicate**	**(I) concurrent**
(J) integrity The quality of being honest and strong about what you believe to be right.	**(K) fluctuate** (for prices and amounts) To keep changing and becoming higher and lower.	**(L) inevitable** Certain to happen and impossible to avoid.
(M) practitioner Someone who works as a doctor or a lawyer.	**(N) simulate** To make or produce something that is not real but has the appearance or feeling of being real.	**(O) intrinsic** Being part of the nature or character of someone or something.
(P) criterion (*noun*) A standard you use to judge something or make a decision about something. *'The college's criterion for success is its exam pass rate'*	**(Q) underlie** (*verb*) To be the cause of something, or be the basic thing from which something develop. *'Social problems underlie much of the crime in big cities'*	**(R) arbitrary** (*adjective*) Decided or arrange without any reason or plan, often unfairly. *'The fees we were charged were completely arbitrary'*
(S) thesis (*noun*) An idea or opinion about something, that you discuss in a formal way and give examples. *'The research supported the thesis that women are better drivers than men'*	**(T) restrain** (*verb*) To control or limit something that is increasing too much. *'Price rises and lower wages usually restrain consumer spending'*	**(U) inherent** (*adjective*) A quality that is a natural part of something and cannot be separated from it. *'Every business has its own inherent risks'*

Unit 11 *Three of a kind*

When the illness first appeared, doctors **suspected** pneumonia.	The analysis of DNA from the crime scene led to the arrest of a _____.	People are often unnecessarily _____ of strangers.
The students here are allowed to **decide** which subjects to study.	I gave several reasons for my _____ to leave the course.	I'm not very _____, even when offered two very simple choices.
When we **compare** the two tables, we can see a lot of differences.	In _____ with his last book, this one is much better.	A _____ study of the two cities shows the many differences between them.
The organisation was widely **perceived** as being too large and disorganised.	Children's _____ of the world are often determined by the behaviour of those around them.	She was a very _____ young woman who understood how people felt and what they were thinking.
A very **long** and detailed report highlighted the difficulties people were facing in the economic crisis.	As the summer days _____, people tend to go out more and stay up later.	We measured the _____ and width of the room.
The company had a **committed** group of employees who worked very hard at building its profile.	We had _____ ourselves to the project, so were unable to back out when things went badly.	The teacher was surprised at the _____ and dedication shown by his students.
We were offered a number of **constructive** suggestions which helped us to improve our performance.	Some IELTS students find it quite difficult to _____ a good argument when writing.	When people could no longer afford new housing, the _____ industry suffered considerably.
The snow had a **predictable** effect on public transport, with train and bus services cancelled across the city.	Nobody could _____ the terrible effect the disease would have on the population.	The data from the research can be used to make _____ about future climate patterns.
Memory loss is often a part of **ageing**.	As people _____, they become slower at learning.	His parents died when he was young, and he was brought up by an _____ aunt.
I'm sorry, but I have a terrible **memory** for names. Who are you?	He _____ the entire speech, so didn't have to refer to his notes when speaking.	The pianist gave a _____ performance which people will remember for a long time.
The government refused to consider the **legalisation** of drugs.	Abortion used to be against the law, but it was _____ in the 1960s.	In some countries, carrying an identification card is a _____ requirement.
In all animals, there is a complex **interaction** between the mind and the body.	Some children are unable to _____ well with other children because they lack confidence.	The museum has some _____ exhibits which visitors can touch and play with.

Unit 12 *In other words*

Student A

---

1 Here is your first question: *Do you find learning English difficult?*

Talk for about 1–2 minutes.
Do not use the words **learning, difficult**.

---

2 Here is your second question: *How much influence do teachers have on our lives?*

Talk for about 1–2 minutes.
Do not use the words **influence, lives**.

---

3 Here is your third question: *What are the advantages and disadvantages of using the internet as a learning resource?*

Talk for about 1–2 minutes.
Do not use the words **advantages, disadvantages**.

What was Student B's first question? Complete the sentence.
Describe a subject that you _____ at _____.

What was Student B's second question? Complete the sentence.
Do you find it easy to _____ things you have _____?

What was Student B's third question? Complete the sentence.
Do you think that studying a language is _____ or _____?

- - ✂ - ✂ - - - - - - - - - -

Student B

---

1 Here is your first question: *Describe a subject that you enjoyed at school.*

Talk for about 1–2 minutes.
Do not use the words **enjoyed, school**.

---

2 Here is your second question: *Do you find it easy to remember things you have learnt?*

Talk for about 1–2 minutes.
Do not use the words **remember, learnt**

---

3 Here is your third question: *Do you think that studying a language is interesting or boring?*

Talk for about 1–2 minutes.
Do not use the words **interesting, boring**.

What was Student A's first question? Complete the sentence.
Do you find _____ English _____?

What was Student A's second question? Complete the sentence.
How much _____ do teachers have on our _____?

What was Student A's third question? Complete the sentence.
What are the _____ and _____ of using the Internet as a learning resource?

Unit 13 *Attributive adjectives*

Team A

Here are the words for the other teams in your group:

beliefs   economy   historical   interest   operation   places   role   rural

Here are your sentences:

1 Recent _____ _____ conducted at the North Pole has shown that the Earth is warming up faster than ever before.

2 Crime isn't just a feature of towns, cities and other _____ _____: it is also very common in the countryside.

3 An increasing workload and the stress that results from this can have a very _____ _____ on people's physical and psychological health

4 The results of the survey were made public because it was felt they would be of _____ _____ to ordinary members of the public.

Team B

Here are the words for the other teams in your group:

agricultural   areas   complicated   general   important   land   public   scientific

Here are your sentences:

1 It is generally accepted that _____ _____ have a much higher standard of living than those which are less developed.

2 The _____ _____ depends on workers who can move easily from farm to farm at different times of the year.

3 Stonehenge and Avebury, which are two ancient stone circles in Britain, are places of great _____ _____.

4 Most people would agree that it is wrong to discriminate against people because of their _____ _____ or the colour of their skin.

Team C

Here are the words for the other teams in your group:

countries   effect   industrialised   interest   negative   religious   research   urban

Here are your sentences:

1 As more houses are built in the countryside and valuable _____ _____ is lost as a result, the country relies more and more on imported food.

2 Schools are vital for learning subjects like maths and languages, but parents also play an _____ _____ in their child's learning.

3 In 2007, smoking was banned in shopping centres, bars, clubs, restaurants and other _____ _____.

4 A heart transplant (giving one person another person's heart) is an extremely _____ _____ which requires a great deal of skill.

PHOTOCOPIABLE

Unit 14 *Mistake match-up*

Student A

(1)	In the current economical climate, we must keep costs to a minimum.	G
(2)	I really enjoy speaking English, but I often have problems with my pronounciation, and I find long words particularly difficult.	
(3)	Despite plenty of evidence that the man was guilty, the police was unable to make an arrest.	
(4)	Saltzburg, which is one of the most beautiful cities in Austria, is famous for it's connections with Mozart.	
(5)	While the number of crimes has risen in the last few years, there has been a significant decrease of the number of violent crimes.	
(6)	I prefer to spend my evenings indoors watching the television, and rarely go out or see my friends.	
(7)	Petrol fumes from motor vehicles are seen often as the main cause of air pollution.	
(8)	The town what I grew up was one of the most polluted places in the country.	
(9)	There are many young people believe that the easiest way to succeed in life is to become famous, even though very few achieve this.	
(10)	I live in London since I was a boy, and have only left the city two or three times to visit relatives in the countryside.	

--- ✂ ---

Student B

(A)	Fast food is extremely popular, but it is also very unhealthy as it does not generally include fruit or vegetable's.	
(B)	We were assured that we would have a lovely weather, but it rained non-stop for almost two weeks.	
(C)	The beginner's course lasts for ten weeks, and in the end of it students take a test to find out if they can move up to the next level.	
(D)	It is becoming difficult increasingly to find places where you can escape from the noise of people and traffic.	
(E)	The United Nations (often simply referred to as the UN) is an international organisation that were established in 1945.	
(F)	People start learning a language later in life find it much more difficult than those who start young.	
(G)	He graduated from university, and afterwards a year travelling around the world, found a job as a tour guide.	1
(H)	After the motorway has been built in 1957, people started to rely more on cars and less on public transport.	
(I)	Istanbul, where is one of the world's largest cities, has a population of over 15 million.	
(J)	Unfortunatly there is no 'magic bullet' for health, and perhaps the best way to avoid illness is to lead a healthy lifestyle.	

Unit 15 *Something in common*

achieve	break	confirm	enter	erupt	establish	find	give	let	listen	lose	make
prepare	promise	reach	say	talk	travel						

1 You should _____ your booking by phone or email at least two weeks in advance. (6th letter)

2 Attempts have been made _____ links with other universities worldwide. (3rd letter)

3 _____ bread, you need flour, water, salt and yeast. (3rd letter)

4 Local farmers refused _____ their land be used for testing genetically modified crops. (3rd letter)

5 Our teacher made us all _____ to hand in our homework first thing on Monday morning. (4th letter)

6 He denied _____ my favourite cup, even though he was the last person to use it. (1st letter)

7 You have an excellent chance of _____ a good score in the IELTS. (5th letter)

8 The volcano could _____ at any moment. (2nd letter)

9 Scientists are finally _____ out why some people are immune to the disease. (1st letter)

10 Without backing up files, you risk _____ all your work if the computer crashes. (2nd letter)

11 The team was _____ across the Sahara when they became lost. (2nd letter)

12 He worked extremely hard and the company decided _____ him a pay rise (3rd letter)

13 There wasn't enough information for the research team _____ a satisfactory conclusion. (4th letter)

14 Upon _____ the country, all visitors are given a traditional welcome. (3rd letter)

15 People who regularly enjoy _____ to music are twice as likely to describe themselves as 'generally happy' than those who don't. (3rd letter)

16 _____ during the exam is strictly prohibited. (1st letter)

17 I think it's too early for me _____ whether or not the project will succeed. (2nd letter)

18 The team ate a special high energy diet while _____ for the Olympics. (1st letter)

The 'mystery' words are _ _ _ _ _ _ _ _, _ _ _ _ _ _ and _ _ _ _.

Unit 16 *Total evaluation*

predictably	worryingly	surprisingly
unlikely	hopefully	ridiculous
clearly	unusually	totally
barely	rather	fortunately
interestingly	significantly	essential

1 He was lying to everyone. (*There was no doubt he was lying to everyone*)	**2** Hot tea is a refreshing drink on a hot day. (*Most people don't expect tea to be a refreshing drink on a hot day*)	**3** The effects of the illness are reduced following a course of anti-viral drugs. (*The effects of the illness are reduced quite a lot*)
4 The results of the survey into crime were depressing. (*Everyone knew the results would be depressing*)	**5** Cleaner sources of fuel will be found in the near future. (*You are optimistic about this*)	**6** Technology often brings solutions to the problems it creates. (*You believe this is lucky*)
7 Dolphins can swim and sleep at the same time. (*You think this fact is interesting*)	**8** Levels of some pollutants in the water supply are high. (*You are anxious about this*)	**9** It was a hot day for early June. (*You don't normally expect this*)
10 Humans will travel to planets outside our solar system within the next 20 years. (*You don't think this will happen*).	**11** You should review the vocabulary you learn on a regular basis. (*You think this is extremely important*)	**12** Don't assume that men are better drivers than women. (*You think it very unreasonable to assume this*)
13 He was 18 when he made his first million dollars. (*You want to emphasise how young he was at that point*)	**14** We were exhausted when we returned home. (*You want to emphasise how exhausted you were*)	**15** Most people thought the new product was expensive. (*People felt the product was a bit too expensive*)

Unit 17 *More or less a crossword*

_all	_alloon	_essen	_estrict	_hrink	_iden	_iminish
_oost	_prawl	_pread	_rop	_scalate	_urge	_windle

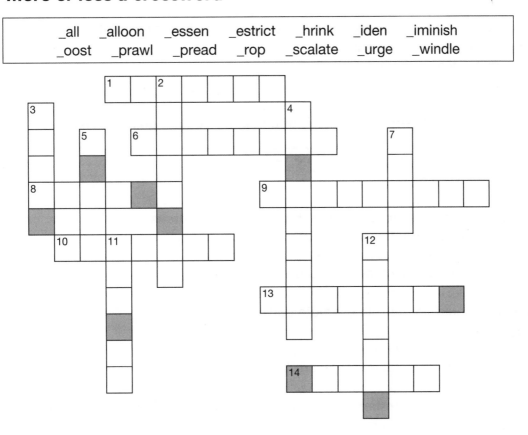

Across:

1 From just a few metres across in the town, the river has **w**_____ to 2 kilometres by the time it reaches the sea.

6 Too much negative criticism can **d**_____ motivation.

8 Only ten minutes after it had started, the fire had **s**_____ through the whole building

9 Unemployment **b**_____ from 3% to over 30% in just six months.

10 Everyone knows that exercise **l**_____ the risk of heart disease.

13 It is doubtful whether new 'fat' taxes will **r**_____ the sale of unhealthy food.

14 Holiday prices have **f**_____ by almost 20% in the last three years.

Down:

2 The elephant population has **d**_____ since the beginning of the century.

3 I believe that a new holiday resort would **b**_____ tourism in the area.

4 People worry that if crime **e**_____ any further, law and order will break down completely.

5 As the water levels began to **s**_____, people made plans to evacuate their homes.

7 Temperatures **d**_____ rapidly at night in the desert.

11 The town's population has **s**_____ since 1990, and now there are only three families living there.

12 The city is enormous and **s**_____ for miles.

Rearrange the letters in the shaded spaces to make a new word that will complete this sentence:

The population of the school _ _ _ _ _ _ _ _ _ _ around 120 children
(= *the population of the school keeps changing, becoming higher and lower*).

Unit 18 *What do you think?*

Tourism rarely benefits the people who are *supposed* to benefit from it.
Do you agree with this statement?
Speaking time (to nearest 30 seconds): _____.
Did they give a convincing argument? (score 1–5): _____.

How important is it to learn the language of a country you are going to visit?
Speaking time (to nearest 30 seconds): _____.
Did they give a convincing argument? (score 1–5): _____.

Tourism does far more harm than good to popular destinations.
How far do you agree with this statement?
Speaking time (to nearest 30 seconds): _____.
Did they give a convincing argument? (score 1–5): _____.

Governments should do more to promote eco-tourism.
Do you agree?
Speaking time (to nearest 30 seconds): _____.
Did they give a convincing argument? (score 1–5): _____.

How important is it to understand the culture of a country you are going to visit.
Speaking time (to nearest 30 seconds): _____.
Did they give a convincing argument? (score 1–5): _____.

Do you agree that tourists should adapt to the culture and traditions of the country they are visiting, and not the other way round.
Speaking time (to nearest 30 seconds): _____.
Did they give a convincing argument? (score 1–5): _____.

The more you travel, the more you accept people from different cultures.
Is this an accurate statement?
Speaking time (to nearest 30 seconds): _____.
Did they give a convincing argument? (score 1–5): _____.

There is no such thing as a 'bad' travel experience: even when things go wrong, we benefit from that experience. Would you agree?
Speaking time (to nearest 30 seconds): _____.
Did they give a convincing argument? (score 1–5): _____.

Do you think that everybody should spend a year of their lives living in another country?
Speaking time (to nearest 30 seconds): _____.
Did they give a convincing argument? (score 1–5): _____.

Travelling abroad makes you appreciate your own country much more.
How far do you agree with this statement?
Speaking time (to nearest 30 seconds): _____.
Did they give a convincing argument? (score 1–5): _____.

Unit 19 *Four in a row*

1 Many working women rely _____ relatives to help take care of their children.
2 Research has provided new insights _____ the way we process language.
3 _____ common with many cities, London has serious pollution problems.
4 Of the three methods used to test intelligence, the first stood _____ as the most reliable.
5 The King's Highway runs _____ the desert from Amman to the Red Sea.
6 A recent photograph should be attached _____ your application form.
7 He only weighed 2 kilos _____ birth, and it seemed unlikely he would survive.
8 Our ability to tell right from wrong usually begins _____ infancy.
9 The temperature varies _____ 10 and 15 degrees Celsius.
10 Much of her early work was centred _____ the development of the internet.
11 Some people are not very good _____ saying *No*.
12 Their mission was to seek _____ new planets and new civilisations.
13 Despite two months of treatment, there was little evidence _____ any change in her condition
14 _____ the whole, I was very pleased with my results.
15 Seen from space, the river appears _____ a thin brown line.
16 If a smile goes _____ longer than 10 seconds, it is probably not genuine.
17 The key _____ success is hard work and perseverance.
18 Her anger was a response _____ the conditions under which she was working.
19 Out _____ guilt, he bought everyone expensive presents.
20 The police asked us lots of difficult questions, probing _____ the truth.
21 Scientists laugh _____ the idea that you can tell a person's character from their face.
22 Some people are liable _____ apologise for something, even if they are not to blame for it.
23 The people trapped _____ the building were finally rescued.
24 Don't forget to put a full stop _____ the end of the sentence.
25 Crime is often associated _____ poverty.
26 A brief smile flickered _____ his face when I told him what had happened.
27 The volcanic eruption was accompanied _____ a powerful earthquake.
28 When you are in a busy place, it is important to be aware of the people _____ you.
29 Too much unhealthy food in childhood can cause serious problems later _____ life.
30 Embarrassment _____ your face is a non-verbal way of saying you regret something.

Unit 20 *The write stuff*

(A) Describing an object
(B) Describing changes (from a table or graph)
(C) Comparing similarities and differences
   (from a table or graph)
(D) Describing a process
(E) Expressing an opinion
(F) Concluding an argument

balance   believe   Compared   conclusion
consists   divided   During   eventually
gradually   identical   levelled   lower
lowest   many   Meanwhile   more   opinion
peak   point   shape   stage   steady
sum   summarise   then   Therefore   things
trend   unlikely   which

		START			
(1) The environment is in trouble, but I _____ we can all do something about it.	**(2)** Life expectancy in developing countries is much _____ than that in industrialised nations.	**(3)** The ingredients are _____ to those in other products.	**(4)** _____, in the final analysis, people are highly motivated by money.	**(5)** First, the bread is baked and _____ it is left to cool.	**(6)** There was a steady downward _____ in both sectors.
(7) This is a device _____ prevents ships getting lost at sea.		**(8)** In my _____, the gap between rich and poor is unavoidable.	**(9)** This device _____ of three main sections.		**(10)** _____ with country A, which is largely rural, over three-quarters of the population live in urban areas.
(11) To _____, in most cases the educational system needs to be improved.	**(12)** In _____, people need to eat more healthily.	**(13)** The number of visitors increased _____ over the period.	**(14)** The country with the _____ rate of heart disease is Japan.	**(15)** From my _____ of view, there are not enough good TV programmes for children.	**(16)** House sales reached a _____ in 2007.
(17) Prices _____ out briefly before rising again.	**(18)** The image is recorded on the memory card. _____ this process, other essential data is also added.			**(19)** The machine is _____ into four main parts.	**(20)** The machine heats up and at this _____ the computer takes over.
(21) The way I see _____, it is impractical to do more than one job well.	**(22)** Doctors in the city have twice as _____ patients as those in the countryside.	**(23)** It is rectangular in _____ and made of metal and plastic.	**(24)** I think it is _____ that people will ever stop going to war.	**(25)** It is considerably _____ complex than a radio.	**(26)** On _____, this is a useful book with plenty of practice materials.
(27) Factory fumes pollute the air. _____, industrial waste enters the water system.		**(28)** Production takes a long time, but _____ the goods are ready to be shipped.	**(29)** To _____ up, you should never underestimate the power of the media.		**(30)** Prices remained _____ between 2006 and 2009.

▶ Teacher's Notes

Unit 1 *Personally speaking ...*

Language focus:	Talking about health and fitness / monitoring overuse of 'stalling' devices (e.g. pauses, repetition, pause 'markers').
	Use this activity after *Focus on speaking 1*, p.9 or *Focus on speaking 2*, p.11.
Exam focus:	Speaking (especially Part 3).
Type of activity:	Speaking activity based on talking continuously for a set time limit on a given topic.
Time:	About 15–20 minutes.
Organisation:	Pairs.
Preparation:	Make one copy of the activity for each student pair in the class. Cut into cards.

1 Divide the class into pairs and give each pair a set of cards, which they should place face down between them. Tell them to look at the top card.

2 Explain to students that this card, and each of the other cards, contains a typical question that they might encounter in the IELTS Speaking Test. These questions are related to the theme of *health and fitness*. Explain that they are going to ask each other these questions, and must respond to the questions they are asked. They will need to speak for 2 minutes for each question they are asked.

3 While students are speaking, they should pay attention to the pause 'markers' and other features that are listed in **bold** under the question. Students should try to avoid overusing these*. Each time they do this, their partner will tick one of the boxes on the card. If their partner ticks both boxes next to one of the markers, they must stop speaking.

(* Note that this includes 'repetition': students repeating the same idea, often using different words. This sometimes happens towards the end of the time allowed for a student to speak in an exam, when they have run out of things to say but feel they need to fill in the time.)

Ask students to return the card they have been looking at to the set.

4 Students then start the activity, with one student playing the part of the interviewer. The interviewer turns over the top card, asks their partner the question and monitors them to check they don't overuse the features marked in **bold***. The interviewer

should time their partner for 2 minutes. Students then swap roles and this process is repeated for about 15 minutes. Each student should have the same number of questions to answer; they are not expected to use up all of the cards.

5 The student in each pair who is able to answer the most questions without overusing the 'pause' markers or without pausing for 5 seconds more than once is the winner.

Unit 2 *Perfect pairs*

Language focus:	Linking in and between sentences.
	Use this activity after *Focus on writing 2*, p.25, ex. 4.
Exam focus:	Writing (general).
Type of activity:	Competitive gap-fill activity.
Time:	About 10–15 minutes.
Organisation:	Groups of four, divided into teams of two.
Preparation:	Make two copies of the activity for each group of four students in the class.

1 Divide the class into groups of four, and ask each group to divide into teams of two. Give each team a copy of the activity. Ask them to skim the main text to get a general understanding of what it is about, but do not let them do anything else yet. They should not worry about the gaps at this stage.

2 Explain (or elicit) that the words missing from the text are 'linking' words used in and between sentences. At this point, remind students of the importance of good linking in the IELTS exam, and ask them why it is important, e.g. it creates better cohesion and coherence, which makes the message they are conveying easy to understand and easy for the reader to follow.

3 Each missing word is numbered and lettered: 1A and 1B, 2A and 2B, etc.

The table under the text has the words that are needed to complete the text. These words are in pairs, lettered A and B. There are 6 word pairs that will not complete any of the gaps in the text.

4 Each student team in a group should take it in turns to choose a pair of words in the table that can fill in two adjoining gaps in the text. They then write those words in the gaps in the text, and delete the words from the table.

5 The teams continue to do this until they have completed all of the gaps in the text, or until they are unable to complete any more gaps (which will happen if one of the teams chooses an incorrect word pair from the table). Alternatively, set a time limit of 10 minutes to do the activity, then tell the class to stop playing.

Before students do the activity, check that they understand the procedure. If necessary, do the first two with them.

6 Review students' answers. The team with the most correct answers in each group is the winner.

Key

(**1A**) whereas / (**1B**) they　(**2A**) Despite / (**2B**) well
(**3A**) such / (**3B**) us　(**4A**) which / (**4B**) where
(**5A**) First / (**5B**) the　(**6A**) then / (**6B**) and
(**7A**) This / (**7B**) which　(**8A**) addition / (**8B**) it
(**9A**) These / (**9B**) order　(**10A**) because /
(**10B**) which　(**11A**) While / (**11B**) this　(**12A**) soon /
(**12B**) and　(**13A**) When / (**13B**) they
(**14A**) but / (**14B**) that

Unit 3 *Give us a word*

Language focus:	Formal vs informal language.
	Use this activity after *Academic Style 2*, p.36.
Exam focus:	Writing (general).
Type of activity:	Competitive word-exchange/gap fill.
Time:	15–20 minutes.
Organisation:	Groups of four, divided into teams of two.
Preparation:	Make one copy of the activity for each group of four students in the class. Cut into two sections: Team A and Team B.

1 Divide the class into groups of four, and ask each group to divide into teams of two. Give each team a copy of either the Team A or Team B section of the activity.

2 Explain to students that they all have sentences about an imaginary city. The sentences on the left of their table (the 'A' sentences) use words and expressions that might be considered *informal* and *inappropriate* in a piece of written IELTS work. Remind students that IELTS writing tasks are more academic than other writing tasks such as informal letters, stories,

etc., which feature in other exams, and they are expected to be able to use appropriate – i.e. more formal – language. The sentences on the right (the 'B' sentences') have the same meaning, but use more formal language. However, some of the words have been removed.

Tell students that the words in the box underneath the table are not the words they need to complete their 'B' sentences: they are the words that the other team need to complete theirs.

3 Allow students a few minutes to read through their sentences. They should discuss in their teams which words they think can be used to complete their sentences, and write their best guess in the margin to the right of each sentence.

4 The two teams in each group then take it in turns to give their opposing team the words in their box, one word at a time. Each time they are given a word, they should write it in the correct place in the appropriate sentence. If they don't know where it can go yet they should write it down on a separate piece of paper. They can then use the word later when they think they know where it should go (the more words they have, the easier it will be for them to identify where each word goes).

5 Set a time limit of 15 minutes for the activity. Tell the class when they have 5 minutes left, and again when they have 1 minute left.

6 Review answers. The team in each group with the most words in the correct places is the winner.

Key

Team A

The city **lies** between the Black Mountains and the Bay of Tranquility.

Since 1990, more than three million people have **moved to** the city from the countryside.

The population **rapidly increased / increased rapidly** in the early 21st century.

The city **is the most highly populated** in the world.

There is **severe** overcrowding in the suburbs.

The population **is estimated to be** about ten million.

It can be **quite difficult** finding somewhere to live.

The city is a **popular** tourist **destination**.

Team B

There **is insufficient accommodation** for people moving to the city.

Unsurprisingly, the city is badly polluted.

The cost of living in the city is becoming **increasingly** expensive.

The city **is famous for** its beautiful parks and gardens.

It has been said that there are more parks here than in any other city in the world.

The restaurants in the city **are claimed to be** the best in the country.

There are many restaurants in the city. **However**, they are very expensive.

The high prices are **the result of** the high prices restaurant owners have to pay for rent.

Unit 4 *Two cities*

Language focus:	Language of contrast and comparison.
	Use this activity after *Focus on writing*, p.41, ex. 7.
Exam focus:	Writing Task 1.
Type of activity:	Sharing information to fill in a table and find a new 'hidden' word.
Time:	About 15 minutes.
Organisation:	Pairwork.
Preparation:	Make one copy of the activity for each student pair in the class. Cut into two sections: Part 1 and Part 2. Cut Part 1 into two cards: Student A and Student B.

1 Divide the class into pairs, and give each student a Student A or Student B card. They should not show these to each other.

2 Explain to students that their cards show prices, costs, etc., for two cities called Gallio and Moesia. Working together, they should compare these various prices, costs, etc. They should do this by asking and answering questions. For example, *What's the average salary in your city?* With the information they have, they should then verbally compare the two cities. For example: *So, average salaries in both cities are more or less the same.* Allow them about 5 minutes to do this.

3 Give Students Part 2 of the activity. Explain that sentences a) –h) can be completed with between 1 and 3 words, and that these words should be written in

the table at the bottom of the page. The numbers in brackets at the end of each sentence indicate where in the grid these words should be written. Students should still not show their Student A/B cards to each other.

Alternatively, to make this more challenging, you could ask students to return their Student A/B cards so that they have to complete the information from memory. Tell them in Step 2 above that they should try to remember as much information as possible.

4 If students do this activity correctly, they will reveal a 'hidden' word in the shaded vertical column. This word, which can be used when comparing two things, places, objects, etc. can be used to complete the sentence in the box.

5 The first pair in the class to reveal this word is the winner.

6 Students can follow this activity up by working in their pairs and writing a short essay on the two cities. They should do this in the style of IELTS Writing Task 1, using at least 150 words. Alternatively, they could do it individually as a homework task.

Key

1 under 2 times 3 half 4 four 5 three
6 quarter 7 nearly 8 identical 9 little
10 approximately 11 exactly 12 just 13 twice

The word in the shaded vertical column is *differentiate*.

Unit 5 *Top topics*

Language focus:	Writing and identifying facts and opinions on different subjects.
	Use this activity after *Focus on reading 2*, p.55, ex. 2.
Exam focus:	General: reading and writing skills.
Type of activity:	Writing about a subject, and deciding what other students have written about based on what you read.
Time:	20 minutes+, depending on the size of the class.
Organisation:	Pairwork and whole-class activity.
Preparation:	Make one copy of the activity and cut into cards.

1 On the board, write the following sentences:

1 Some people say that factors such as noise and pollution in a _____ can have a strong negative impact on the inhabitants.

2 As has been frequently demonstrated, people who live in a _____ are more suspicious of strangers.

3 According to the latest statistics, 60% of _____ residents have been a victim of crime.

4 However, research findings indicate that _____ life is not as stressful as many think.

Explain to students that the missing word in each sentence is the same. Ask students what they think that word is (*city* is the best answer).

Ask them if they can tell you anything else about the sentences. Elicit the fact that the first sentence gives an opinion, and the other three give facts. The language and structures are based on exercise 2 on page 55 of the Student's Book.

2 Divide the class into pairs or groups of three, and give each pair/group in the class one of the cards* (which they should not show to anyone else).

(*If there are fewer than 20 students in your class, you will not need all of the cards.)

3 Tell the pairs/groups to look at the topic word in **bold** on their card, and to read the instructions below it. Their task is to write four sentences incorporating the word they have been given. They should not write the word itself (they leave a gap), and each sentence should contain language used to present either a fact or an opinion (using some of the expressions on page 55 of their Student's Book). Note that the sentences do not need to be linked (i.e. they do not need to follow on from one another to form a single piece of text). Allow them about 8–10 minutes for this. Monitor them and point out any mistakes they might have made that could cause confusion for the reader.

4 Ask the pairs/group to then pass their sentences around the class. Each pair/group should look at all of the other pair/group's sentences and decide: a) what the missing topic word might be and b) how many facts and opinions are given. They should write these down on a separate sheet of paper, e.g. *Group 1: Sport. 3 facts, 1 opinion.*

5 When students have looked at each other's sentences, review their answers. Each time a student pair/group's topic is identified by another pair/group, they get 1 point. They also get 1 point each time a fact or opinion is clearly identified.

Unit 6 *Silent bingo*

Language focus:	Dictionary work. Pronunciation: word stress.
	Use this activity after *Focus on Vocabulary*, p.59, ex. 4.
Exam focus:	Speaking (general).
Type of activity:	Bingo-style activity based on matching words with their stress patterns.
Time:	20–25 minutes.
Organisation:	Pairwork and whole-class activity.
Preparation:	Make one copy of the activity for each student pair in the class. Students will also need dictionaries.

1 Divide the class into pairs and give each pair a copy of the activity.

2 Tell students to look at the words in the box and choose 18 of these words. At this stage, do not tell them why, or what they are going to do with these words. Allow students about 3–4 minutes for this, then ask them to write their chosen words into the spaces on the two grids: one word per space. Students will need to leave a bit of space below each word, as they will be adding more information.

3 While students are doing step 2, draw the following on the board. It should be easy for all of the students to see the difference in size between the two circles (suggest you use the whole of the board).

oO Oo Ooo oOo oOoo ooOoo

4 Ask students to find the words they have chosen in their dictionaries, and to note the position of the stressed syllable in each one. Students then read the words they have chosen to each other, paying particular attention to the position of the stress in each word.

5 Now tell students that they are going to play a game of bingo. The symbols you have drawn on the board show the number of syllables in a word: one circle is one syllable, and the large circle shows which syllable is stressed. You point, at random, to the symbols on the board, pausing for about 30 seconds between each one (see the answers below for guidance). Each time you point at one of the symbols, students should look at their first bingo grid (Game 1), and try to identify one word that uses that syllable/stress pattern. If they find a word, they draw the pattern below it (note that they can only choose one word at a time, even if they have more than one word on their grid that uses the same pattern).

6 As soon as students have drawn symbols below each word on the first grid, they shout *Bingo!* Check their answers: if they are correct they win. If they have made a mistake, the game continues.

7 Repeat steps 5 and 6 for the second game.

8 Some of the stress patterns in this activity are practised at a later stage in the coursebook, so students should not worry if they do not get them all correct. However, this activity should make them aware of the importance of using a dictionary to check pronunciation, and you should encourage them to do so when necessary. At this stage, you could ask students about some of the other benefits of using a good monolingual dictionary (such as the *Longman Dictionary of Contemporary English*). For example, the words are shown in context, comparisons are made with words of similar or opposite meanings, alternative words are given in thesaurus-style boxes, etc.

Key

oO	achieve assign assist aware commence locate obtain occur resource
Oo	challenge conscious error factor feature patient quiet scenic
Ooo	accurate argument benefit clarify contribute demonstrate general institute logical maximise physical previous regulate sociable
oOo	athletic cerebral creative determined initial strategic
oOoo	activity administrate adventurous alternative competitive economy environment intelligent particular significant
ooOoo	analytical unavailable

Unit 7 *Noun phrase risk*

Language focus:	Noun phrases. Use this activity after *Academic Style 3* and *4*, p.56 and 76,
Exam focus:	General.
Type of activity:	Competitive gap-fill based on rewriting sentences using appropriate noun phrases.
Time:	20 minutes.
Organisation:	Small group and whole-class activity.
Preparation:	Make one copy of the activity for each group of three/four students in the class.

1 Divide the class into groups of three or four, and give each group a copy of the activity.

2 Explain to students that the second sentence (B) in each sentence pair can be completed with words

---

from the box, so that it includes or forms part of a noun phrase, and so that the main meaning is similar to sentence (A). In groups, students should try to complete as many of these as possible in 15 minutes.

3 When the time is up, students should decide how certain they are that their answers are correct. They do this by risking points, shown at the bottom of the activity sheet. For each answer, students should write the number of points they are prepared to risk in the right-hand column. Allow them about 3–4 minutes for this. Do the first one as an example so that everyone understands how this works.

4 Review answers. Each group begins with 100 points. If an answer is correct, students add on the number of points they risked. If an answer is wrong, they remove the number of points they risked.

5 The winning group is the group with the most points when all the answers have been reviewed.

Key

1 fossil fuels **2** Information technology **3** rush hour **4** language barrier **5** agreement about the **6** worry about the **7** cost of living **8** point of view **9** the discovery of **10** our dependence on

---

Unit 8 *In a nutshell*

Language focus:	Developing an argument – either *evidence-led* or *thesis-led* – in response to a given topic. Use this activity after *Critical Thinking 2*, p.87.
Exam focus:	Writing Task 2.
Type of activity:	Group/class writing and topic-development activity.
Time:	25 minutes.
Organisation:	Group and whole-class activity.
Preparation:	Make one copy of the activity and cut into five cards.

Before you begin, review the two types of written argument (thesis-led and topic-led) from *Critical Thinking 2*, page 87. Write a question on the board, e.g. *City life is better than country life. How far do you agree with this statement?* and tell the class to imagine this is a question they must answer in the IELTS writing test. Ask them to give you a thesis-led statement or an evidence-led statement to begin the essay.

1 Divide the class into five groups, and give each group one of the cards. Ask one student in each group to read the statement and question out loud to the group.

2 Explain to students that these statements and questions are typical of argument-style writing questions. In the space below, they are going to briefly answer the topic as follows:

Students have a time limit of 3 minutes to write a sentence next to number 1 on their card. This sentence must either be (a) a thesis statement (in which case, they are presenting a *thesis-led* argument), or it must be (b) a factual point (in which case they are presenting an *evidence-led* argument). Monitor the groups, and try to help any who are struggling to come up with an idea. Extend the 3 minute time limit if necessary.

When the 3 minutes is up, you will call out *change!* and students pass their card to another group. That group should then continue the argument next to number 2 on the card. They will need to pay particular attention to the first sentence, as this will determine the style and content of their sentence.

Repeat this until all the groups have written one sentence on each of the cards. Before students write their last sentence, they should look at the previous sentences very carefully and if the first sentence is not a thesis-led statement, they must include it here.

3 Ask one student in each group to read out all of the sentences on the card they have completed. The class can then discuss which argument was more effective, and whether it would have been better to have made the argument *thesis-led* or *evidence-led*.

As a follow-up, students could develop the sentences on their card into an essay. They might decide to keep the sentences they already have as a single paragraph forming the introduction (although it would be unusual to have an opening paragraph of more than three or four sentences), or they could break it up and incorporate some of the sentences into a later part of the essay – making sure the opening paragraph contains the thesis statement. This will involve adding more information, and dividing the text into paragraphs. Their final product should be about 250 words long.

Unit 9 *Double-decker dominoes*

Language focus:	Adjectives (especially derived adjectives) and their endings.
	Use this activity after *Focus on vocabulary*, p.95, ex. 3.
Exam focus:	General.
Type of activity:	Domino-style matching game.
Time:	About 15 minutes.
Organisation:	Pairs or small groups of three.
Preparation:	Make one copy of the activity for each pair or group in the class. Cut into cards. Shuffle each set well.

Before you begin, check that students are familiar with the game of dominoes. Illustrate a short example on the board if necessary. Explain that they are going to play a new version of this game.

1 Divide the class into pairs (or groups of three) and give each pair a set of cards.

2 Tell students to find the two 'Start' cards and put them face-up on their desk. Place the Start card marked 'Top card' above the Start card marked 'Bottom card', so that they can see both cards.

3 Point out that the Start card marked 'Top card' has a sentence on it, including part of a word in **bold**, and the Start card marked 'Bottom card' has a dictionary definition of the same word (taken, or adapted, from the *Longman Exams Dictionary*). Ask students to think of the correct suffix to complete the word and to write it on a separate piece of paper.

4 Once students have completed the word, they need to find an adjective on the left-hand side of another card that uses the same *suffix*. For example, if the completed word on the <u>right</u> side of the card ends in -*ic*, the completed word on the <u>left</u> side of another card must also end in -*ic*. Students should place this card next to the 'Start' card, and find the matching definition on a shaded card.

If necessary, illustrate steps 2–4 with the first two cards: both *academic* and *symbolic* end in -*ic*, so these cards go together.

5 Students repeat steps 3 and 4 until they have joined all their cards together. The winner is the pair who a) correctly join all their top and bottom cards and b) complete the adjectives with the correct letters.

6 If you have time, ask students to use the words in sentences of their own.

Key

The cards are in their correct order on the activity page. The words are: academic + symbolic, respiratory + migratory, unreliable + sustainable, appropriate + inadequate, ecological + psychological, varied + integrated, controversial + beneficial, global + municipal, urban + equestrian.

Unit 10 *Total recall*

Language focus:	Reflective learning: recording and remembering vocabulary.
	Use this activity after *Reflective Learning 3*, p.107.
Exam focus:	General.
Type of activity:	Memory activity.
Time:	About 15–20 minutes.
Organisation:	Groups of three.
Preparation:	Make one copy of the activity for each group of three in the class. Cut into cards.
	Students will also need dictionaries (ideally the *Longman Exams Dictionary*): one copy per group of three.

1 Divide the class into groups of three and give each group a dictionary (if they don't have their own) and the first three cards only (containing the words *subsidy, convene* and *predominant*). They should ignore the letters at the beginning of each card. Ask students, in their groups, to write down a) the part of speech of each word, e.g. *noun, verb* or *adjective*, b) a definition for each word (in English or their own language) and c) a sample sentence. Students should use their dictionary for this, and write the information on the card (using the back if necessary). Allow them about 5 minutes for this.

2 On a separate sheet of paper, ask each student to write down the letters A–U.

3 Give each group the other cards. Ask them to add the cards that they wrote on to this set, shuffle them and put them on the desk between them (face up or face down).

4 Now ask students to look carefully at all of the cards: some of them just show a word, some show a word and its definition (or one possible definition in the case of words that can have more than one meaning), and others show a word, its definition and a sample sentence (including the cards they wrote on). All of the words come from the *Academic Word List*. As they look at each card, they should tick off the letter on their sheet (this is just a check list, so they know they have looked at all of the cards). Allow them about 10 minutes to do this.

5 When students have looked at all of their cards, ask them to return their cards to you, and turn their paper over. They now have 90 seconds to write down as many words as they can remember. Students only need to write the words not the definitions, and they can be in any order. At this stage, each student should work on his/her own, and not as part of a group.

6 Ask students to think of which words they remembered, and why they think this is.

In most cases, students will have remembered all of the words they wrote definitions for (and these will probably appear at the top of their list), most of the words for which there were definitions and sample sentences, fewer for those where there were just definitions, and fewer still where only the word was shown (and these should mostly appear at the end of their list).

Ask students what they can learn from this in terms of recording and remembering vocabulary. Possible suggestions include the importance of seeing/learning a word in context, the importance of writing down new vocabulary items, and the importance of giving as much information as practically and reasonably possible when recording that item. Ask if there are any ways they could improve this system, e.g. by adding a translation in their language, drawing a picture, etc. Ask students what other aspects of a word are important to know, e.g. pronunciation, grammar (past tense/past participle, dependent prepositions, etc.), register, collocations, etc. You should also stress the importance of contextualising vocabulary when recording it, and recycling that vocabulary as much as possible.

Unit 11 *Three of a kind*

Language focus:	Word families: noun, verb and adjective forms of the same words.
	Use this activity after *Focus on vocabulary*, p.113.
Exam focus:	General.
Type of activity:	Card collection/sentence completion game.
Time:	About 15 minutes.
Organisation:	Groups of four.
Preparation:	Make one copy of the activity for each group of four students in the class. Cut into cards, and divide into two sets: the cards with the words in **bold**, and the cards with the gapped sentences. Shuffle both sets of cards.

1 Divide the class into groups of four, and ask each group to divide into teams of two. Give each group a set of the cards with the **bold** words. Explain to students that these words are all taken from Unit 11 of the Students' Book and/or from the *Academic Word List*. Ask students to read each one, then shuffle them and place them face down between them. Each pair should then take 6 of these cards.

2 Now give each group the gapped cards, which they should place face down between them. Explain to students that these cards contain sentences with a missing word. These missing words should be other forms of the words in **bold** on the cards they are already holding (for example, if one of the bold words on one of their cards is a *noun*, there are two other cards in the set that should contain another form – a *verb* and an *adjective* – of that word). The aim of the activity is to collect the other two cards that match the cards they are already holding. In other words, they are collecting sets of three cards that use the same 'stem' word. They will need to identify the cards they need from the context of the sentence.

3 One team in each group begins by turning over the top card and reading out the gapped sentence. If they, or the other team in their group, thinks the missing word is another form of the word on one of their cards, they claim it for themselves.

4 Step 3 is repeated for 10 minutes. At this stage, tell students to stop playing. Ask them if either team in their group managed to collect any 'sets' of three cards (their original card and two from the gapped cards). The student teams should award themselves 5 points for each set collected.

5 Students now have 5 minutes to complete the gaps on their cards with the correct form of the missing word. When the time is up, review their answers. The student teams should then award themselves an extra point for each correct word. The winner is the pair in each group with the most points.

As a follow on, you might like to point out to students that many of their words have more than one meaning, depending on the context in which they are used. Ask them if they can identify any of these.

Key

The sets are together on the activity sheet

Set 1: suspected, suspect, suspicious

Set 2: decide, decision, decisive

Set 3: compare, comparison, comparative

Set 4: perceived, perceptions, perceptive

Set 5: long, lengthen, length

Set 6: committed, committed, commitment

Set 7: constructive, construct, construction

Set 8: predictable, predict, predictions

Set 9: ageing, age, aged

Set 10: memory, memorised, memorable

Set 11: legalisation, legalised, legal

Set 12: interaction, interact, interactive

Unit 12 *In other words*

Language focus:	Speaking (with emphasis on answering a question clearly, concisely and accurately) and listening. Paraphrasing. Use this activity after *Focus on speaking 2*, p.124.
Exam focus:	Speaking (especially the Long turn section).
Type of activity:	'Taboo' style speaking game.
Time:	15–20 minutes.
Organisation:	Pairwork.
Preparation:	Make one copy of the activity for each student pair in the class. Cut into two sections, Student A and Student B.

1 Divide the class into teams of two, and give each student a Student A or Student B section of the activity. They should not show these to each other.

2 Explain to students that the boxes on their paper contain three questions (similar to the sort of questions they might be asked in the 'Long turn' section of the IELTS Speaking test), and that they are going to answer them. Each question is followed by a time indicator (1–2 minutes in each case), and two words that they are not allowed to use when speaking. Let students look at their questions for 2 minutes, and think about how they might answer them. In particular, students should think of how they might rephrase or paraphrase the words they are not allowed to use.

3 Both students then take it in turns to answer their questions, speaking clearly so that their partner can hear them. Explain that it is very important they do not deviate from the subject, add extra, unnecessary information, or fail to answer the question.

4 When the time allocated for each question is up, their partner then looks at the gapped sentences at the bottom of their paper. From the talk they have just heard, they should decide what those missing words are, and write them in the spaces.

5 When students have finished all of their questions, they should compare their answers with each other and award their team points (1 point for each word they identified, giving a maximum of 12 points for both students). In some cases, alternative answers may be acceptable, e.g. *studying* instead of *learning*, etc. Students should check with you if they are not sure.

6 The winner is the team with the most points.

Unit 13 *Attributive adjectives*

Language focus:	Review and practice of attributive adjectives (classifying, topical and evaluative). Use this activity after *Academic Style 7*, p.136.
Exam focus:	Writing (general).
Type of activity:	Competitive word-exchange/gap-fill activity.
Time:	15 minutes.
Organisation:	Groups of three.
Preparation:	Make one copy of the activity for each group of three students in the class. Cut into three cards, Student A, Student B and Student C.

1 Divide the class into groups of six, and ask each group to divide into three teams of two. Give each team a Team A, Team B or Team C card. They should not show these to the other teams in their group.

2 Ask each team to read out the words in **bold** to the other teams in their group. If students are in any doubt about the pronunciation of their words, they should ask you for help or (ideally) check in a dictionary. The other teams should listen carefully, but they should not make notes.

3 Ask students what kinds of words they read out/ heard, i.e. what parts of speech they were, and elicit the fact that they were nouns and adjectives (and, specifically, attributive adjectives). Check that students remember what attributive adjectives are. If not, ask them to look back at *Academic Style 7*, page 137 before they begin. Remind students about the importance of attributive adjectives in academic English.

4 Now explain to students that each of their four sentences can be completed with a combination of an attributive adjective and a noun. These words are all being 'held' by the other two teams, i.e. the words that were read out in Step 2. They must try to 'obtain' these words from those teams. They do this as follows:

Each team takes it in turns to ask another team to repeat one of the words they read out in Step 2.

That team reads out one word from their list. If the 'asking' team thinks that word fits into one of their sentences, they write it there. They tell the 'reading' team they have 'accepted' that word, and the reading team must delete that word from their list: they cannot read it out again. If they do not accept the word, the 'reading' team do not delete the word from their list.

This is repeated for 10–15 minutes. When this time is up, tell students to stop playing and review their answers. The teams should award themselves 1 point for each word they have correctly used in their sentences. They then add up their points, the winner being the team in each group with the most points.

In many of the sentences, other words may be possible to complete the gaps. When the activity is over, you could ask students for more suitable collocations. For example, *historical importance*, *simple operation*, etc.

Key

Team A: **1** scientific research   **2** urban areas
3 negative effect   **4** general interest

Team B: **1** industrialised countries   **2** rural economy
3 historical interest   **4** religious beliefs

Team C: **1** agricultural land   **2** important role
3 public places   **4** complicated operation

Unit 14 *Mistake match-up*

Language focus:	Error identification and correction. Use this activity after *Reflective Learning 4*, p.147.
Exam focus:	General, but especially Writing.
Type of activity:	Sentence matching game.
Time:	20 minutes.
Organisation:	Pairwork.
Preparation:	Make one copy of the activity for each student pair in the class, and cut into two sections (Student A and Student B).

Before you begin, review the main categories of mistakes (see the list in *Reflective Learning 4*, page 147). Using the abbreviations there is both an efficient way of carrying out this task and very useful practice for your students.

1 Divide the class into pairs, and give each student a Student A or Student B section.

2 Explain that the ten sentences on their paper all contain a mistake. Each of the mistakes on their paper is related in some way to a mistake on their partner's paper. Tell them to look at the example that has been done for them: ask one of the Student A's to read out their sentence (1), and ask one of the Student B's to read out their sentence (G). Elicit the fact that in both cases, a wrong word form has been used: Student A's *economical* should be *economic*, and Student B's *afterwards* should be *after*.

3 Working together, but without looking at each other's papers, students should try to 'match' the other sentences. They should do this by identifying the mistakes in their own sentences, correcting them, then asking their partner if they have a similar type of mistake. Students then write the matching sentence's number/letter on the right side of their table (1 = G, 2 = E, etc.).

4 The first pair in the class to match all of their sentences/mistakes is the winner. Alternatively, set a time limit of 10–12 minutes, and if no one has matched all of their sentences when the time is up, allow them another 5 minutes to continue the activity, this time looking at each other's sentences.

Key

1 G **WW**

2 J **Sp** (2) pronunciation; (J) Unfortunately

3 E **S -> V** (3) '… the police <u>were</u> …'; (E) '… that <u>was</u> established …')

4 A **P** (4) <u>its</u> connections; (A) vegetables (no apostrophe in either case)

5 C **Prep** (5) decrease <u>in</u>; (C) <u>at</u> the end of it

6 B **A** (6) watching ~~the~~ television; (B) ~~a~~ lovely weather

7 D **WO** (7) are <u>often seen</u>; (D) <u>increasingly difficult</u>

8 I **Coh** (wrong relative pronoun) (8) town <u>where</u>; (I) Istanbul <u>which</u>

9 F **Coh** (missing relative pronoun) (9) people <u>who</u> believe; (F) People <u>who</u>

10 H **T** (10) I <u>have lived</u>; (H) the motorway <u>had</u> been built

Unit 15 *Something in common*

Language focus:	-*ing* and infinitive forms.
	This activity supports the grammar in the *Key Language Bank*, p. 230, ex. 28, and can be done after students have done the exercises there.
Exam focus:	General.
Type of activity:	Gap-fill, revealing 'mystery' words.
Time:	15 minutes.
Organisation:	Pairwork or small groups.
Preparation:	Make one copy of the activity for each pair or small group of students in the class.

1 Divide the class into pairs or small groups, and give each group a copy of the activity.

2 Explain to students that each of the sentences can be completed with a form of the words in the box. In some cases, this will be an -*ing* form, in some cases it will be an infinitive with *to*, and in some cases it will be an infinitive without *to*. The sentences all follow the rules provided in the Key Language Bank, p. 230, ex. 28.

3 In pairs/groups, students should complete the sentences. They should then take the letters of the word, which is indicated after each sentence, and write these in the spaces at the bottom of their sheet. For example, if the answer to a sentence is *to get*, and the letter indicated is the 4th letter, they should write *e* at the bottom of the page. In some cases, more than one answer may be possible, so there is a partial element of chance in this activity.

4 If students do this correctly, they should reveal three 'mystery' words. Apart from being verbs, these words have something in common. Your students should decide what this is (answer: the words are *remember*, *forget* and *stop*, and can all be followed by either an -*ing* or an infinitive form verb (with *to*), depending on how they are used*). The first pair/group to identify this common factor is the winner. Students might find a dictionary useful here: the *Longman Exams Dictionary* is particularly useful, as the entry for *remember* has a box which illustrates the two possible uses.

* Examples:

Did you remember to lock the door? / I clearly remember shutting the door and locking it.

I forgot to post your letter. / I forget calling her, but she reminded me of it this morning.

He was really busy, but he stopped to get a coffee. / His headaches became less frequent when he stopped drinking coffee.

Key

1 confirm   **2** to establish   **3** To make   **4** to let
5 promise   **6** breaking   **7** achieving   **8** erupt
9 finding   **10** losing   **11** travelling   **12** to get
13 to reach   **14** entering   **15** listening   **16** Talking
17 to say   **18** preparing

Unit 16 *Total evaluation*

Language focus:	Critical thinking: language of evaluation.
	Use this activity after *Critical Thinking 4*, p.167.
Exam focus:	Writing (general).
Type of activity:	Card game with sentence-writing element.
Time:	20–25 minutes.
Organisation:	Groups of three.
Preparation:	Make one copy of the activity for each group of three students in the class. Cut into two sets of cards (the small word cards and the larger sentence cards).

Before you begin the activity, do the following:
On the board, write the following, and ask students to note how the word *naturally* is incorporated into the second sentence so that it reflects the attitude of the speaker (shown in brackets at the end of the first sentence):

He was intelligent and ambitious, so succeeded at everything he did. (*You expected him to succeed at everything he did*).

naturally

He was intelligent and ambitious, so **naturally** succeeded at everything he did.

With the class, review some other evaluation-style structures, based on the above example. For example, **It is easy to see why he succeeded at everything he did**. Refer students back to *Critical Thinking 4* to give them more ideas.

1 Divide the class into groups of three or four, and give each group the two sets of cards, which they should place face down between them.

2 Tell each group to take one of the large cards, turn it over, and read the sentence. This follows the same format as the first sentence on the board (i.e. a fact, followed by the speaker's attitude in brackets). They are going to rewrite that sentence, basing it on the speaker's attitude, and using words which they will find on the small cards.

3 One student in the group then starts turning over the small cards, one at a time, and reading or showing the words to the others in their group. If one student in the group thinks a word can be used to rewrite the sentence on their large card (as in the second sentence on the board), they say *stop*, and tell the others in the

group why and how the word can be used. If they agree, the group then works together to incorporate that word in a new version of the sentence on the large card. They can write the 'new' sentence on the back of the large card. Sometimes the word will go in the sentence, sometimes it will start the sentence, and sometimes it will form part of a longer phrase which will go at the beginning of the sentence.

4 When the sentence has been written, the large card and small card are placed to one side, and steps 2 and 3 are repeated.

5 After about 10–15 minutes, tell the class to stop playing. Review answers, giving each group a point for each correct sentence they have written. The winning group is the group in the class with the most correct sentences.

Key

These are the best answers, although your students may come up with others, e.g. *It was a **surprisingly** hot day for early June.* You should decide if their sentences are correct when you review their answers.

1 He was **clearly** lying to everyone.

2 Hot tea is a **surprisingly** refreshing drink on a hot day.

3 The effects of the illness are **significantly** reduced following a course of anti-viral drugs.

4 The results of the survey into crime were **predictably** depressing.

5 **Hopefully**, cleaner sources of fuel will be found in the near future.

6 **Fortunately**, technology often brings solutions to the problems it creates.

7 **Interestingly**, dolphins can swim and sleep at the same time.

8 Levels of some pollutants in the water supply are **worryingly** high.

9 It was **an unusually** hot day for early June.

10 **It is unlikely that** humans will travel to planets outside our solar system within the next 20 years.

11 **It is essential to** review the vocabulary you learn on a regular basis.

12 **It is ridiculous to** assume that men are better drivers than women.

13 He was **barely** 18 when he made his first million dollars.

14 We were **totally** exhausted when we returned home.

15 Most people thought the product was **rather** expensive.

Unit 17 *More or less a crossword*

Language focus:	'Change' words to describe increasing and decreasing. Use this activity after *Focus on vocabulary*, p.172. ex. 2.
Exam focus:	Writing (especially Task 1).
Type of activity:	Crossword with a 'hidden word' element.
Time:	20 minutes.
Organisation:	Pairs.
Preparation:	Make one copy of the activity for each student pair in the class.

Before you do this activity, briefly review verbs we use to talk about change (page 172). However, make sure students have their Student's Books closed when they do the activity.

1 Divide the class into pairs, and give each pair a copy of the activity.

2 Explain to students that each sentence can be completed with a word describing change. The first letter has been included in the sentence, and the rest of the word can be found in the box above the crossword. However, in some cases, they will need to change the form of the word (e.g. to its past participle form).

3 In pairs, students complete the sentences with the words, and then write their answers in the crossword grid.

4 The letters in the shaded spaces can then be rearranged to make another word associated with change (this will be a new word for them). Students should rearrange these letters to make that word. The winning pair is not the pair to be the first in the class to complete their grid, but the first pair to identify what this word is.

Key

Across:
1 widened   6 diminish   8 spread   9 ballooned
10 lessens   13 restrict   14 fallen

Down:
2 dwindled   3 boost   4 escalates   5 surge   7 drop
11 shrunk   12 sprawls

The word that completes the sentence in the box is *fluctuates*.

Unit 18 *What do you think?*

Language focus:	Speaking: working together to discuss a topic and present an opinion. Use this activity after *Focus on speaking 1*, p.179.
Exam focus:	Speaking (Part 3).
Type of activity:	Competitive speaking on a given topic.
Time:	25 minutes.
Organisation:	Groups/pairs.
Preparation:	Make one copy of the activity for each student pair in the class, and cut into ten cards.

Before you begin the activity, it might be useful for students to review some useful speaking expressions:

- Expressing an opinion (page 39)
- Giving reasons for an opinion (page 124)
- Answering a difficult question (page 149)
- Balancing an argument (page 173)

1 Divide the class into groups of four, and give each group a set of cards. Ask them to read the questions/statements on these cards, and ask them what topic they all have in common (= travel and tourism). When students have looked at all of the cards, ask them to shuffle them and place them face down on their desk.

2 Ask each group to divide into pairs (if you have an uneven number of students, some will have to work in groups of five, divided into a pair and a group of three). Explain to students that they are going to discuss the statements on the cards in their pairs.

3 One pair begins by taking one of the cards and reading the statement/question to the other pair. That pair should have a few moments to collect their thoughts, and then they should start discussing it together. The idea is to keep talking for as long as possible* until they have no more to say on the subject, sticking to the topic and without repetition of ideas.

(* You could set a time limit of 3–4 minutes for each discussion.)

4 As soon as students start talking, the pair that gave them the statement/question starts timing them, and when they finish speaking, they write down how long they spoke (to the nearest 30 seconds). They should also write down how convincing they thought the argument was, and how relevant their conversation was to the statement. (1 is the least convincing/relevant, 5 is the most convincing/most relevant).